Foucault

JOSÉ GUILHERME MERQUIOR was a professional diplomat, a university teacher, a scholar and a thinker, and a prolific writer. He was born in Rio de Janeiro in 1941, and studied law and philosophy in Brazil before undertaking postgraduate work in Europe. Among his many publications are *The Veil and the Mask: Essays on Culture and Ideology* (1979), *Rousseau and Weber* (1986) and *From Prague to Paris: a critique of structuralist and poststructuralist thought* (1986).

Modern Masters

Foucault

Second Edition

J. G. Merquior

![FontanaPress]
FontanaPress
An Imprint of HarperCollins*Publishers*

Fontana Press
An Imprint of HarperCollins*Publishers*
77–85 Fulham Palace Road
Hammersmith, London, W6 8JB

This second edition published by Fontana Press 1991
9 8 7 6 5 4 3

First published in Great Britain by
Fontana 1985

ISBN 0 00 686226 8

Printed and bound by
Caledonian International Book Manufacturing Ltd, Scotland

This book is for the Atalanta

Contents

Acknowledgements

By attempting a highly original merger of philosophy and history, Michel Foucault set out to revitalize philosophical reflection through several provocative analyses of the Western past. In assessing the results of his bold historico-philosophical enterprise, I have taken into account all his main published texts, including the last volumes, yet untranslated, of his unfinished *History of Sexuality*. I have tried in earnest to give as fair a hearing as possible to his views, but in the end my own assessment was prompted by a reluctance to accept what Robert Weimann has so aptly called 'the trend towards aestheticizing history', as well as by more than one misgiving about the overall direction of post-structuralist thought. The tenor of my critique has benefited a great deal from conversations with John A. Hall, Ernest Gellner, Guita Ionescu, Perry Anderson and Raymond Boudon, among others. Pierre Nora and Nicole Evrard graciously procured for me, before publication, the second and third volumes of the *History of Sexuality*. Helen Fraser was a great help in getting rid of many an awkwardness of expression in the original draft. My wife Hilda took loving care of an often tortured manuscript, and my daughter Julia composed with charming zest the bibliography, which was located or detected to a large extent through the goodwill of Ophelia Vesentini and Paula Tourinho. Carminha C. Fernandes compiled the index. As for Frank Kermode, he was the most responsive of editors; if this book has earned me anything valuable, it has been the privilege of his friendship.

JGM
London, May 1985

It is a mark of a higher culture to value the little unpretentious truths, which have been found by means of strict method, more highly than the joy-diffusing and dazzling errors which spring from metaphysical and artistic times and peoples.

Nietzsche

1. The historian of the present

I have never been a Freudian, I have never been a Marxist and I have never been a structuralist.

Michel Foucault

When Michel Foucault died in Paris of a cerebral tumour in June 1984, *Le Monde* printed an obituary by Paul Veyne, the distinguished classical historian and Foucault's colleague at the Collège de France. He declared Foucault's work 'the most important event in thought of our century' (*l'évènement de pensée le plus important de notre siècle*). Few would agree with Veyne's bombastic claim; yet his hero doubtless died as one of the most influential thinkers of our time.

Foucault may not have been the greatest thinker of our age, but he was certainly the central figure of French philosophy since Sartre. Now the French way of doing modern philosophy has long been something quite different from what is normally seen as standard practice in the Anglo-Saxon world – at least until yesterday. 'Normal' English-speaking philosophy is generally both academic in style and analytic in method. The point is worth stressing because some continental brands of modern philosophical thought, notably in German-speaking areas, have been as academic – often in a ponderous manner – as their English counterpart without, however, being tightly analytic in the sense that Russell and Wittgenstein or Ryle and Austin were, and that most living Anglo-Saxon thinkers such as Quine still are. By contrast, the most prestigious philosophizing in France took a very dissimilar path.

One might say that it all began with Henri Bergson. Born in 1859, Bergson was an exact contemporary of the initiator of modern philosophy in Germany, Edmund Husserl; and like Husserl, he had a long teaching career – but his works grew increasingly essayistic in form, while his lectures were attended by crowds and he himself became a kind of cult figure. No sooner had he died (in 1941) than a new philosophical guru with a highly literary style emerged in the person of Jean-Paul Sartre (1905–80), the unrivalled (though not unchallenged) superstar of French thought up to the 1960s. Like Bergson, he combined brilliant literary gifts with a theorizing wantonly free of analytic discipline. It was to this tradition of philosophical glamour rather than rigour that Foucault belonged.

It would be grossly unfair to suggest that all Gallic philosophy in the twentieth century stems from such alluring loose practice, which one is tempted to call 'litero-philosophy'. Nevertheless, in no other modern philosophical culture do we find this kind of thinker in such prominence. Moreover, French litero-philosophy was a mixed genre of sorts. It seldom took an overt literary form, such as Nietzsche dared to give it. Rather, it usually put on an aspect of far staider inquiries, as in Bergson's *Creative Evolution* (1907), or even of treatises, like Sartre's *Being and Nothingness* (1943) or Merleau-Ponty's *Phenomenology of Perception* (1945). However, in the eyes of a philosophical public brought up in the analytic framework (or again, in the solemn jargons of mainstream German theory) the end result was much the same.

Now Foucault's point of departure seems linked with a subtle change in the fortunes of litero-philosophy. It was as though, after the exhaustion of existentialism (and the later Sartre's misguided attempt to blend it with Marxism), litero-philosophy underwent a period of inner doubt. Apparently, the ebbing of the anguish-and-commitment syndrome in the more detached intellectual atmosphere under de Gaulle's Fifth Republic threw such a theoretical genre into considerable disarray. As a consequence, French philosophy came to face, as it were, a choice: either it converted itself to analyticalness (since the appropriation of German themes, chiefly from Husserl and Heidegger, had already been achieved by existentialism) or it devised a new strategy for its own survival. In the process, the brightest of young philosophers opted for the second alternative. Instead of making philosophy more rigorous, they decided to make it feed on the growing prestige of the 'human sciences' (e.g., linguistics, structural anthropology, the history studies of the Annales school, Freudian psychology) as well as of avant-garde art and literature. Thus literophilosophy managed to regain vitality *by annexing new contents*, borrowed from other intellectual provinces.

Outstanding among these new thinkers were Michel Foucault and Jacques Derrida. Derrida's 'grammatology' (later rechristened 'deconstruction') defined itself as a radical reprise of Saussure's theory of structural linguistics. As to Foucault, he turned to history, but with a keen eye to some fascinating uncharted territories within the Western past: the evolution of social attitudes toward madness, the history of proto-modern medicine, the conceptual underground of biology, linguistics and economics. In so doing, Foucault quickly acquired the reputation – alongside the anthropologist Claude Lévi-Strauss, the literary critic Roland Barthes, and the psychoanalyst Jacques Lacan – of being one of the tetrarchs of structuralism, the intellectual fashion which rose amidst the ruins of existential philosophy. Then, he shared with Derrida the leadership of 'poststructuralism', that is, of the love-hate relationship with the structuralist mind which came to prevail, in Parisian culture, from the late 1960s on.

Foucault was a complex, almost elusive intellectual personality. Perhaps his single most notorious statement remains the ominous proclamation of the 'death of man' at the close of *Les Mots et les choses*, the bold 'archaeology' of cognitive structures that brought him into the limelight since the mid-sixties. Nevertheless the cool elegance of this never-abjured anti-humanist detachment did not prevent him from doting on California as a counterculture paradise, nor indeed from performing a romantic denigration, as passionate as that attempted by Herbert Marcuse, of Western reason. Alone of all the structuralist pantheon fully to have shared the spirit of May 1968, Foucault was a polite professor who relished scandalizing the Parisian establishment which lionized him by solemnly stating that the first duty of prisoners was to try to escape, or again by enthusiastically supporting the Ayatollah Khomeini's revolutionary breakout in the teeth of all leftist pieties. His actions were those of an odd radical much as his writings were those of a maverick structuralist; so maverick that – as shown in our epigraph – he bluntly refused the structuralist label.

This book is a critical essay on his work. I shall strive not only to give a fair hearing to all his main texts but also to examine a fair amount of the literature on him. At the same time, I shall try to explain the shifts and changes of his thought until his very last works – the final volumes of his *History of Sexuality* (1976–84). Then, by way of conclusion, some tentative light will be cast on the ultimate stand of the man who tried hard to place post-structuralism on an ethico-political ground, at a far remove from the textual navel-gazing of 'deconstruction'.

Foucault was born in Poitiers into a middle-class family. His father, a doctor, sent him to a Catholic school. By the end of the war young Michel had become a boarder at the Lycée Henri IV in Paris, bracing himself for the entrance exam to one of the French *grandes écoles*, the Ecole Normale Supérieure. There, and at the Sorbonne, he studied under Jean Hyppolite, the translator and interpreter of Hegel's *Phenomenology of Mind*, as well as under the historian of science, Georges Canguilhem, and the future founder of structuralist Marxism, Louis Althusser. He emerged as a *normalien* at twenty-three, the same year in which he received his diploma of philosophy. He joined the Communist party but broke with it in 1951. Within a year, dissatisfied with philosophy, Foucault, who had also a formal education in psychology, turned to psychopathology, the field in which he was to publish his first book, *Maladie Mentale et Psychologie* (1954). For four years he taught at the French department of the University of Uppsala, then was appointed director of the French institutes of Warsaw and Hamburg. While in Germany he completed his long study on the history of madness which earned him his *doctorat d'état*.

In 1960, he became head of the philosophy department at the University of Clermont-Ferrand in Auvergne, where he stayed until glory took him to Paris following the publication, in 1966, under the prestigious seal of Gallimard, of *Les Mots et les choses*, a born-classic of structuralism in its heyday. In the late 1960s he taught philosophy at the avant-garde university of Vincennes and in 1970 was given the chair of history of systems of thought at the Collège de France – a position previously held by Hyppolite. Alongside his professorships Foucault did a lot of lecturing and exhibited some gauchiste militancy: he edited the leftist weekly, *Libération*, spurred on penal reforms through his Groupe d'Information sur les Prisons, and came forward on behalf of the gay movement. In countless interviews, he also proved to be, of all the structuralist masters, the most outspoken polemicist, vigorously counter-attacking criticism from *maîtres-à-penser* such as Sartre or younger challengers such as Derrida.

How did Foucault describe his own philosophy? On one occasion, replying to Sartre's criticisms, Foucault went so far as to suggest that structuralism as a category existed only for outsiders, for those who did not belong to it.[1] He meant, of course, that the 'tetrarchy' ruling over French thought in the sixties (a pentarchy if one includes Louis Althusser, the master of structuralism *in partibus fidelium*, i.e., in Marxland), formed no coherent group. In the foreword to the English edition (1970) of what passes for his typical structuralist book, *The Order of Things*, he protested that although some 'half-witted commentators' in France had dubbed him a structuralist, he used 'none of the methods, concepts or key terms that characterize structural analysis'.

Still, there is at least one positive Foucaldian definition of structuralism. Right at the middle of *The Order of Things*, he calls structuralism 'the restless consciousness of modern knowledge'. Since then he often said that his aim was to write 'the history of the present'.[2] To find the conceptual underpinnings of some key practices in modern culture, placing them in historical perspective: such is the purpose of all the main books by Foucault published in the twenty-odd years from *Madness and Civilization* to *The History of Sexuality*, the completion of which was to be published posthumously.

Their author was a thinker who died while still in his middle age. Born in 1926, Foucault belongs to the generation of Noam Chomsky (b. 1928), Leszek Kolakowski (b. 1927), Hilary Putnam (b. 1926) and Ernest Gellner (b. 1925). He was a little younger than John Rawls (b. 1921) or Thomas Kuhn (b. 1922), a bit older than Jürgen

Habermas (b. 1929) or Jacques Derrida (b. 1930), but considerably older than Saul Kripke (b. 1940). These constitute, admittedly, a motley crowd in contemporary thought, but it is they who, since the mid-sixties and early seventies, in many different ways, have so altered the philosophical landscape as to challenge the vintage 1900 – 10 class – the class of Popper, Gadamer and Quine – as the main shapers of our conceptual outlook (outside, that is, the scientific realm). To the general public, half, at most, of these younger thinkers already enjoy fame; and Foucault seems second only to Chomsky (not a philosopher by background) as a true celebrity among them all. Why?

The main reason for the impact of Foucault seems to lie in the very content of his work. A discourse on power and on the power of discourse – what could be more attractive to intellectuals and humanities departments with an increasingly entrenched radical outlook, yet who have also grown sick and tired of the traditional pieties of left revolutionism? At the root of Foucault's large readership there is the swell of intellectual and academic *schismaticism*, which by and large survived the ebbing of student revolt throughout the last decade. Michel Foucault was a philosopher who placed an unusual kind of learning (what humanist today can discuss Port-Royal grammar, naturalists before Darwin, or the prehistory of the modern prison system?), uncommon gifts as a writer and, last but not least, remarkable rhetorical skills at the service of ideas and assumptions highly palatable to broad sectors of the Western intelligentsia, helping decisively to forge these very notions in the process. This is what remains fundamentally at stake in his concern with a critical 'history of the present'.

Let us now sketch – as a working hypothesis with which to begin a critical analysis of his thought – a broad characterization of his philosophical programme. We have seen Foucault describing himself as a historian of the present. Indeed, for many students of continental philosophy he is *the thinker who welded philosophy and history* and in so doing developed a dazzling critique of modern civilization.

In his last years Foucault often spelt out his project of a historico-philosophical critique of modernity by suggesting that it comprised two distinct goals: one was the identification of the 'historical conditions' of the rise of reason in the West; the other is 'an analysis of the present moment' seeking to check how we *now* stand, vis-à-vis the historical foundation of *rationality* as the spirit of modern culture.

Modern philosophy, he explains, largely derives from the will to inquire into the historical emergence of 'adult' autonomous reason. Its theme is, then, the history of reason, of rationality in the great forms of science, technology and political organization. To that extent, it hinges upon Kant's celebrated question, 'What is the Enlightenment?' (1784), to which Foucault referred in a number of texts. Very perceptively, he remarked that in France since Comte the Kantian question had been translated into 'What is the history of science?' whereas in Germany it took another form: from Max Weber to Habermas's 'critical theory' it faced the problem of *social* rationality. As for himself, Foucault saw his contribution as a shift within the French traditional concern with *reason as knowledge*: 'While historians of science in France were interested essentially in the problem of how a scientific object is constituted, the question I asked myself was this: how is it that the human subject took itself as the object of possible knowledge? Through what forms of rationality and historical conditions? And finally at what price? This is my question: at what price can subjects speak the truth about themselves?'[3]

For Descartes, it may be remembered, the fact that the human subject can take itself as its own object was precisely the beginning of solid knowledge. But to Foucault, as to the structuralists, this would simply beg the question. For if there is one thing upon which they agree, it is that the idea of a founding, grounding subject ought to be abandoned, since (they claim) it implies the primacy of a transparent consciousness and a fatal neglect of what structuralism is after: hidden, unconscious determinations of thought. Thus the founding subject – the royal theme of idealism, from Descartes to Hegel – becomes the *bête noire* of structuralism. In his slightly dull 'methodological' treatise, *The Archaeology of Knowledge* (1969), Foucault made no bones about it: his task, he wrote, 'to free the history of thought from its subjection to transcendence'. Whose transcendence? Well, first and foremost, that of the hated subject:

My aim was to analyse history in the discontinuity that no teleology would reduce in advance; [...] to allow it to be deployed in an anonymity on which no transcendental constitution would impose the form of the subject; to open it up to a temporality that would not promise the return of any dawn. My aim was to cleanse it of all transcendental narcissism.[4]

A few pages further on, he pleads innocent of the charge that structuralism ignores history by claiming that he never denied the possibility of discourse change ('discourse' being his word for thought as a social practice); all he did was to deprive 'the sovereignty of the subject' of the 'exclusive and instantaneous right' to make change, i.e., to originate history.

What exactly does Foucault mean? Some commentators found the vow to free thought from transcendence both extravagant and obscure.[5] Foucault's use of words is definitely poles apart from the cautiousness of analytical philosophy. We seem to enter firmer ground as the quote proceeds to an exorcism of 'teleology' in historical knowledge. Here 'transcendental narcissism', the self-contemplating subject, appears to be pointing at what gave historicism such a bad name: its propensity to uphold unwarranted logics of history, imposed on the historical record rather than deduced from it. Is that really what Foucault, in his attempt at grasping the prehistory of the present in several social practices, from social science and psychiatry to our handling of criminals and our idea of sexuality, is getting at? Is this the starting point in his philosophical history?

Foucault hinted at the convenience of deeming his project of a history of the present as some sort of synthesis between the two lines of inquiry – French and German – derived from the Kantian question on the Enlightenment, namely, on the nature of modern reason. Of the French line – the (Comtean) theory of reason as history of science – Foucault made a selective use: he retained the focus on reason *as knowledge*, yet relinquished the (positivist) view of science as the embodiment of an objective and universal reason. But Foucault also praised the German line – the (Weberian) theory of reason as social rationality – for its alertness to the variety of social forms of reason.

He praised its pluralist concept, as it were, of rationality in modern culture – and indeed tended to misconstrue Weber's focus on social embodiments of rationality as a licence for an overtly relativist view of history – a blatant oversimplification of Weber's complex stance. Be that as it may, Foucault confessed to sharing the Weberian-Frankfurtian curiosity about 'the different (social) forms' taken by the 'ascendancy of reason' in the West. Reminiscing about his university years, he regretted that France knew so little of Weberian thought[6] (a slight exaggeration, since by that time sociologists such as Raymond Aron or philosophers such as Merleau-Ponty already knew their Weber very well – but let it pass).

Clearly, Foucault beckons us to see his own enterprise as an attempt at conducting an inquiry into modern rationality which entails a probing of the foundations of social science ('How is it that the human subject took itself as the object of possible knowledge?'). This, in turn, should be pursued without losing sight of a whole 'ensemble of complex, staggered elements' involving 'institutional game-playing, class relations, professional conflicts, modalities of knowledge and [...] a whole history of the subject of reason'; for such are, says Foucault, the heterogeneous phenomena he has 'tried to piece back together'[7] as he built his conceptual map for a history in depth of our cultural predicament.

Foucault is the first to acknowledge that such a programme is indeed a tall order, perhaps impossible to accomplish. However, it seems to me that, at least *in principle*, the Foucaldian programme has a merit: it patently tries to dispose of the cloudy notion of a unitary reason echoing the transcendental Subject in the metaphysics of classical idealism. And why is it so important to reject such a metaphysics? It is important, even imperative, because it represents *too anthropomorphic* a view of the world. The first tenet of idealist metaphysics is, in Maurice Mandelbaum's apt words, the belief that 'within natural human experience one can find the clue to an understanding of the ultimate nature of reality'.[8] Note that in the long run, in the history of modern philosophy, this anthropocentric stance has turned out to be far more influential than the other, rather obvious component in any minimal definition of classical idealism, namely, the belief that man – the clue to our grasp of reality – is a spiritual being. For while soon after the death of Hegel in 1831 the spiritual element in idealism succumbed to the assault of the pervasive secularism of nineteenth-century thought, the anthropocentric viewpoint of idealist metaphysics survived vigorously, from Schopenhauer and Nietzsche to Bergson, Heidegger and the later Wittgenstein – all of them philosophers of the human experience, and interpreters of being in all-too-human terms (like Schopenhauer's Will or, ironically, Nietzsche's 'play'). What Gellner said of Hegel – that he gave us a cosy, homely metaphysics, 'an Absolute in braces'[9] – might indeed be extended to characterize a whole philosophical mood, which was the main legacy of German idealism to our culture.

On the eve of the rise of structuralism, continental philosophy was still imbued with this cosy, humanized view of reality. For example, the transcendental subject lived a pampered existence in the care of modern historicism, i.e., of Marxism restored to its pristine Hegelian source by Lukács, with praxis, totality-drunk, in lieu of Spirit; and it also throve in the phenomenological theme of 'living' reason as the foundation to which, overcoming 'the crisis of European sciences' (in the title of Husserl's own testament), modern philosophy was urged to return, thereby regenerating the Western mind. And it goes without saying that, for the reasons we have just mentioned, this transcendental subject was not at all 'transcendental' in a supernatural sense, but simply in the sense of being a grounding clue to the interpretation of reality. Speaking to *Telos* in 1983, Foucault confessed that by 1960 he toyed with both schools of thought, Lukácsian Marxism and phenomenology, before embarking on his own historico-philosophical studies. But eventually he chose to devise a standpoint whence to launch a clear non-idealist inquiry into the history of modern rationality. Has his work lived up to this promise, or did it miscarry, yielding in the process to new forms of crypto-idealism? Before suggesting any answer, we must look at each one of his major studies as a philosopher-historian.

2. The Great Confinement, or *du côté de la folie*

Foucault's first influential book, published in 1961, was a huge tome entitled *Folie et déraison: histoire de la folie à l'âge classique*. An abridged edition, issued in 1964, was translated into English as *Madness and Civilization*. In it Foucault shows that the 'discourse on madness' in the West has known four distinct phases since the Middle Ages.

Whereas in medieval times madness was regarded as holy, in the Renaissance it became identified with a special form of ironical high reason – the wisdom of folly in Erasmus's famous encomium, also present in the way Shakespeare deals with his mad characters and in Cervantes' often sublime foolish knight. The pre-modern ambivalence towards insanity was best expressed in the topos of the Ship of Fools, which haunted the popular imagination in the Renaissance. On the one hand, through the symbolism of the Ship of Fools, the pre-modern West exorcized madness by 'sending' its loonies away. On the other hand, there seemed to be a dim perception of these vessels as 'pilgrimage boats, highly symbolic cargoes of madmen in search of their reason'. Madness, which was not socially feared and often (as in humanist satire or Brueghel's painting) laid bare the nonsense of the world, pointed at a realm of meaning beyond reason – and in so doing, insanity was expelled *but not excised* from society: assigning a functional role to madness, the Renaissance mind kept quite familiar with it. There were many bridges, social and intellectual, between reason and unreason. Renaissance man thought that madness had a share in truth.

Suddenly, towards the mid-seventeenth century, 'madness ceased to be – at the limits of the world, of man, and death – an eschatological figure'. The imaginary ship turned into a dismal hospital. Europe transformed her long-deserted leprosaria into bedlams. Since the end of the Crusades, the decline of leprosy had emptied the lazar houses – but now *moral* lepers would be their inmates:

At the end of the Middle Ages, leprosy disappeared from the Western world. In the margins of the community, at the gates of cities, there stretched wastelands which sickness had ceased to haunt but had left sterile and long uninhabitable. For centuries, these reaches would belong to the non-human. From the fourteenth to the seventeenth century, they would wait, soliciting with strange incantations a new incarnation of disease, another grimace of terror, renewed rites of purification and exclusion. [...] Leprosy withdrew, leaving derelict these low places and these rites which were intended, not to suppress it, but to keep it at a sacred distance, to fix it in an inverse exaltation. What doubtless remained longer than leprosy, and would persist when the lazar houses had been empty for years, were the values and images attached to the figure of the leper as well as the meaning of his exclusion, the social importance of that insistent and fearful figure which was not driven off without first being inscribed within a sacred circle.[1]

The sentences just quoted come from the first chapter of *Madness and Civilization*. They give a fair idea of Foucault's style, in its peculiar blend of erudition and pathos. The literary radiance of his prose brings home what he wants at once to narrate and indict: the *Grand Renfermement* (in the baroque language of the time), the Great Confinement which sought to tame insanity by segregating madmen as an asocial category. For during the 'classical age' in the French (and Foucaldian) sense, corresponding to the seventeenth and eighteenth centuries, madness was sharply isolated from sanity. Lunatics were no longer expelled from society as 'different' people. They became confined in special places and treated together with other kinds of deviants, such as paupers and criminals, even idlers. In Foucault's account, the Puritan ethic of work is not very far from being just a species of a genus: the new high seriousness of classical bourgeoisie.

To the Renaissance, madness was not yet a disease; in the classical age, it became an idle illness. Rationalist reason put unreason under a 'pathological' curse fraught with ethical overtones.

The classical mental hospital had no psychotherapeutic aims: its chief concern, says Foucault (ch. VI), was 'to sever or to "correct"'. But outside hospitals the classical age gave vent to many 'physical cures' of madness, which were remarkable for their brutality disguised as science. The nastiest results derived from attempts as obnoxious as they were ingenious to forestall or destroy the 'corruption of humours'. Madness seen as a form of bodily deterioration was attacked by methods which sought either, externally, to deflect corrupt substances or, internally, to dissolve the corrupting ones. Among the former was the *oleum cephalicum* of a certain Fallowes. This doctor believed that in madness,

> 'black vapors clog the very fine vessels through which the animal spirits must pass'; the blood is thus deprived of direction; it encumbers the veins of the brain where it stagnates, unless it is agitated by a confused movement 'that distracts the ideas'. *Oleum cephalicum* has the advantage of provoking 'little pustules on the head'; they are anointed with oil to keep them from drying out and so that 'the black vapors lodged in the brain' may continue to escape. But burning and cauterizing the body at any point produces the same effect. It was even supposed that diseases of the skin such as scabies, eczema, or smallpox could put an end to a fit of madness; the corruption then left the viscera and the brain, to spread on the surface of the body, where it was released externally. By the end of the century, it became customary to inoculate scabies in the most resistant cases of mania. In his *Instructions* of 1785, addressed to the directors of hospitals, François Doublet recommends that if bleedings, purges, baths, and showers do not cure mania, the use of 'cauters, setons, superficial abscesses, inoculation of scabies' will.[2]

Not all treatments during the classical age were so harsh and so foolish. Besides physical 'therapies', there were many moral recipes, well documented in Foucault's richly illustrated chapter, 'Doctors and patients' – a veritable *tour de force* of descriptive scholarship. But the main point is crystal-clear: in the classical, early modern West madness became a disease – it lost the dignity of being seen as meaningful unreason.

Then, in the late eighteenth century and throughout most of the next one, psychiatric reforms, pioneered by the Quaker William Tuke at the York Retreat and by Philippe Pinel in Paris, severed the insane from the company of criminals and paupers. In Foucault's Marxist view on this point, the poor were no longer confined because thriving industrialism needed manpower and a reserve army of labour. As for the insane, defined as sick people, humans with a blocked psychic development, they were physically liberated (Pinel breaking their chains at the Bicêtre bedlam during the Terror was an emblematic gesture) and placed under a benign educational regime. However, Foucault is convinced that this was done only in order better to capture their *minds* – a task entrusted to the institution of the asylum. Once in the asylum, the insane person, now a patient placed under the authority of the psychiatric discourse, undergoes a deeply psychological 'trial' from which 'one is never released [...] except [...] by remorse'[3] – moral torture becomes the law of reason's tyranny over madness. In the world of the bedlam, argues Foucault, prior to the psychiatric reforms of Pinel *et al.*, the loonies actually enjoyed more freedom than the modern therapies allow them, because 'classical confinement' treatment did not aim at changing their consciousness. Their body was in chains, but their mind had wings – wings later clipped by the despotism of reason.

Thus in the West thought came firmly to seperate reason from unreason. In Foucault's words, the constitution of madness as an illness at the end of the eighteenth century 'broke the dialogue' between reason and insanity. 'The language of psychiatry, [...] a monologue of reason *about* madness, has been established only on the basis of such a silence'. Thereafter 'the life of unreason' shone only in flashes of maverick literature such as that of Hölderlin, Nerval, Nietzsche or Artaud. As for humanitarian psychiatry in the footsteps of Pinel and Tuke, it amounted to no less than 'a gigantic moral imprisonment'. What is more, the asylum mirrors a whole authoritarian structure – that of bourgeois society. It constitutes 'a microcosm in which were symbolized the massive structure of bourgeois society and its values: Family-Child relations, centred on the theme of paternal authority; Transgression-Punishment relations, centred on the theme of immediate justice; Madness-Disorder relations, centred on the theme of social and moral order. It is from these that the physician derived his power to cure.'[4]

Eventually, in our own time, there emerged a fourth way of conceptualizing the reason/unreason relationship. Freud blurred the distinction between sanity and madness by seeing their polarity as bridged by his concept of neurosis. Yet Freud, despite his decisive supersession of the asylum mentality, kept a crucial authoritarian trait in that he surrendered the mentally disturbed to the spell of soul doctors.

Madness and Civilization certainly opens up a legitimate area of research: the investigation of the cultural assumptions underlying the different historical ways of handling a highly disturbing area of human behaviour. In a warm review of the book the imaginative epistemologist Michel Serres called it an 'archaeology of psychiatry', probably one of the first uses of the term in reference to Foucault (who used it himself in the subtitle or title of his next three books). To Serres, *Madness and Civilization* is to the culture of the classical age 'very precisely' (sic) what Nietzsche's *Birth of Tragedy* was to ancient Greek culture: it casts light on the Dionysian element repressed under the Apollonian order: 'on sait enfin de quelles nuits les jours sont entourés,' concludes he with lyrical enthusiasm.[5] Naturally, the warm welcome Foucault received from the anti-psychiatry movement (Laing *et al.*) was a direct response to this orgiastic streak. Reviewers in America were quick to notice the kinship in mood if not in tone or method with the work of Norman Brown (*Life against Death*, 1959) and its strident paean to the primal id.[6] Also *Madness and Civilization* begat a whole progeny of vindications of psychosis – the best-known of which remains Gilles Deleuze and Felix Guattari's *Anti-Oedipus: Capitalism and Schizophrenia* (1972) – all cast in a strong 'counter-cultural' mould.

In examining his first major historico-philosophical study, we need to ask: does Foucault get his history right? Sometimes it is suggested that asking such a question is a mistake. For Foucault came fully to share Nietzsche's dismissal of history's claim to provide neutral objectivity. In 'Nietzsche, genealogy, history' (1971), [7] he pours a Nietzschean contempt on 'the history of the historians' which, striving for neutrality, fancies an implausible 'point of support outside of time'. How much wiser, says Foucault, is Nietzsche's 'genealogy', which 'does not fear to be a perspectival knowledge': it boldly assumes 'the system of its own injustice'.

But to assert the right to do a 'presentist' history, even to practise an *engagé* history does not release the historian from his empirical duties to the data. On the contrary: in order to prove their point, present-centred *histoires à thèse* must try and persuade us of the accuracy of their reading of the past. After all, Foucault himself described his book as 'a history of the economical, political, ideological, and institutional conditions according to which the segregation of the insane was effected during the classical period'.[8] In the foreword to the original edition of his book, Foucault set out to write a history 'of madness itself, in its vivacity, before any capture by (psychiatric) knowledge' – a task, in the sensible remark of Allan Megill, not very dissimilar from orthodox historiography.[9] It is true that later Foucault came to deny he was aiming at a reconstitution of madness as an independent historical referent[10] – but there is no gainsaying that, *at the time*, he had a 'normal' historiographic purpose in mind when he wrote *Madness and Civilization*. He wanted to question previous historical accounts, not to doubt the legitimacy, let alone the possibility, of doing historical research. We can safely conclude, then, that in the young Foucault the 'anti-historian' was not yet in full existence. In its place, there was just a *counter*-historian, that is to say, a historian challenging prevailing interpretations of a given strand of our past: madness. Therefore we are, at last, entitled to an answer as to whether or not Foucault got his history right.

To an important extent he did. Even one of his main critics – Lawrence Stone – grants that Foucault tends to be right in thinking that widespread confinement in the late seventeenth and eighteenth centuries was a step backwards, subjecting mentally deranged people in an indiscriminate way to a harsh treatment previously meted out only to dangerous psychotics.[11] The trouble begins when Foucault (a) stresses the medieval and Renaissance 'dialogue' with madness, by contrast with the segregating attitude towards it in modern, i.e., rationalist times; (b) insists on treating the 'classical age' – the time of the Great Confinement – as *unprecedented* in the nature, and not just the scale, of its handling of lunacy, setting great store by the conversion of leprosaria into mental hospitals and the rise of a 'physiological' conception of madness as illness; and (c) takes the Tuke-Pinel therapies as brand new methods for coping with mental disease and denounces their moral procedures as thoroughly repressive.

In the fifth chapter of his splendid book, *Psycho Politics* (1982), the late Peter Sedgwick pulled the carpet from under several key assumptions in Foucault's historical picture. He showed, for instance, that long before the Great Confinement many insane people had been in custody and undergoing therapy (however primitive) in Europe. There were several hospitals with special accommodation for the mentally ill in towns across the Rhine valley prior to Foucault's classical age. There was a nationwide chain of charitable asylums, specially for the insane, from the *fifteenth* century, in, of all places, Spain – not exactly a society devoted to embracing modern rationalism. Again, various techniques attesting a crude physiological view of mental illness, which in Foucault's model are attributes of the Age of Reason, were actually rife in prerationalist Europe, many stemming from Muslim societies.

Dieting, fasting, bleeding and mild rotation (centrifuging the lunatic into oblivion by mechanical means) were some such techniques, most of which dated back from *ancient* medicine (an epoch, anyway, out of Foucault's purview). Very sensibly, Sedgwick stresses continuities in the medical craft throughout the ages. He does not deny the expansion of the 'medical attitude' under early modern rationalism, but points out that the medical view of madness cannot possibly be simply derived from a pervasive 'bureaucratic rationalism' breaking sharply with an alleged long tradition of permissiveness towards insanity.

H.C. Erik Midelfort has assembled a number of historical points which further undermine much of the ground of *Madness and Civilization*.[11] Midelfort has no quarrel in principle with Foucault's unmasking of the Enlightenment, and so is far from writing as an outraged defender of any rosy chronicle of heroic therapeutic advances. But he also evinces a formidable command of an impressive literature on the history of both madness and psychiatry.

I can only invite the interested reader to go to Midelfort's brilliant synthesis and glean from his rich bibliographic support. But a number of points are worth making at once: (1) there is ample evidence of medieval cruelty towards the insane; (2) in the late Middle Ages and the Renaissance, the mad were already often confined, to cells, jails or even cages; (3) 'dialogue' or no 'dialogue', madness during those times was frequently connected with *sin* – even in the Ship of Fools mythology; and to that extent, it was regarded in a far less benevolent light than that suggested by Foucault (pre-modern minds accepted the reality of madness – 'madness as part of truth' – just as they accepted the reality of sin; but this does not mean that they *valued* madness, any more than sin); (4) as Martin Schrenk (himself a severe critic of Foucault) has shown, early modern madhouses developed from medieval hospitals *and monasteries* rather than as reopened leprosaria; (5) the Great Confinement was primarily aimed not at deviance but *at poverty* – criminal poverty, crazy poverty or just plain poverty; the notion that it heralded (in the name of the rising bourgeoisie) a moral segregation does not bear close scrutiny; (6) at any rate, as stressed by another critic of Foucault, Klaus Doerner (*Madmen and the Bourgeoisie*, 1969) there was no uniform state-controlled confinement: the English and German patterns, for example, strayed greatly from the Louis Quatorzian *Grand Renfermement*; (7) Foucault's periodization seems to me amiss. By the late eighteenth century, confinement of the poor was generally deemed a failure; but it is *then* that confinement of the mad really went ahead, as so conclusively shown in statistics concerning England, France and the United States; (8) Tuke and Pinel did not 'invent' mental illness. Rather, they owe much to prior therapies and often relied also on their methods; (9) moreover, in nineteenth-century England moral treatment was not that central in the medicalization of madness. Far from it: as shown by Andrew Scull, physicians saw Tukean moral therapy as a lay threat to their art, and strove to avoid it or adapt it to their own practice. Once more, Foucault's epochal monoliths crumble before the contradictory wealth of the historical evidence.

Indeed, his grim tale of high-minded medical tyranny is by no means wholly supported by the actual record of therapy in the age of the asylum. David Rothman, a social historian who did innovative research on the development of mental institutions in Jacksonian America, documented a mid-nineteenth-century *withdrawal* from psychiatric to merely custodial methods (*The Discovery of the Asylum*, 1971). Rothman's story chimes perfectly well with the 'therapeutic nihilism' of the age – the medical reluctance to pass from diagnosis to treatment, based on a pessimistic view of medicine's powers (the young Freud, half a century later, still had to fight this medical ideology, long entrenched in Vienna).[13] Now Rothman is by no means suggesting that the custodial (as opposed to the psychiatric) asylum was a good thing. On the contrary, he sees the custodial spirit as tied up with early bourgeois control of 'dangerous' social categories. But if he is right, then what was 'on' as a repressive phenomenon concerning insanity was a medical *passivity*, not the busybody psychiatry that Foucault wants to present as a handmaid of a despotically interventionist, regimenting Reason.

The brunt of Foucault's book is a passionate case against our received wisdom on the humanitarianism of the Enlightenment. Therefore acclaimed experts of that period, among them Lawrence Stone, could scarcely have failed to rise to such a challenge to their own more balanced views.[14] And what are we to think of his idea of the establishment of psychiatry as 'gigantic moral imprisonment'? The truth is that private madhouses and old state asylums used to be scandalously ill-handled and the reforms of pioneers such as Tuke and Pinel, leading to the creation of the first modern mental hospitals, though not so perfectly angelic as it was once thought, were genuine deeds of enlightened philanthropy. Foucault's charge of 'moralizing Sadism', applied to the infancy of psychiatry, is a piece of ideological

melodrama. It is all very well to take one's stand *du côté de la folie* –
except that, in one's eagerness to cast the insane in the role of society's
victims, one may easily forget that they were often deeply unhappy, and
that their plight cried out for therapy. The idea that the education-
rather-than-fetters approach was just a repressive (however unconsciously so) carceral device does not resist critical examination.
Foucault's bourgeoisphobia tends to dismiss Victorian philanthropy
out of hand, but a less biased middle-class humanitarian called
Charles Dickens, appalled as he was by London workhouses, was
greatly impressed – notes Dr J.K. Wing in *Reasoning about Madness*[15]
– by the humane atmosphere of small mental hospitals in America,
where physicians and staff went as far as to share meals with the
patients. It would be unwise to extrapolate from this, and indeed
many other positive testimonies of contempories, an idyllic portrait
of psychiatric humanity; but neither is there any compelling, factually
backed reason to jump to the opposite conclusion and declare that the
full medicalization of madness during the first age of 'bourgeois'
psychiatry was part and parcel of a ghastly (to use an adjective later
sloganized by Foucault) 'carceral' society.

Indeed, since 1969, we possess the natural corrective to Foucault's
Manichaean picture in Klaus Doerner's well-researched 'social history
of insanity and psychiatry' in bourgeois society. Doerner's *Madmen
and the Bourgeoisie*, a comparative study of the British, French and
German experiences, is far from wholly disagreeing with Foucault in
its description of the dawn of psychotherapy (though it points out his
tendency to generalize too much from the French case). Where
Doerner does depart from *Madness and Civilization* is in his
evaluation of it.

Take his terse chapter on Pinel (II,2), or again, the one (I,2) on the
London physician whom he rightly rescues from the shadows of
oblivion as the first to provide a comprehensive approach to
psychiatry, encompassing theory, therapy and the asylum: William
Battie (1704–76).

The methods of enlightened alienists such as Pinel brought about a
decisive shift from the sequestration of the insane to their return to
social visibility in asylums open to the gaze of relatives, psychiatrists

and medical students alike. But whereas Foucault chastises the 'objectifying' slant of the medical gaze at work in the regime of observation under which patients were placed, Doerner stresses that the primacy of 'moral treatments' largely entailed the abandonment of traditional medical methods; and to that extent, amounted to a considerable rejection of the 'distancing attitude' (just remember Dickens's American hospital).

Similarly, Doerner, who has a keen eye for the influence of Rousseaunian ideas on non-authoritarian moral education (Pinel was a devotee of Jean-Jacques) and does not overlook the spread of pre-romantic sensibility on the eve of the psychiatric reforms, finds Battie's cure-not-care programme, in mid-eighteenth-century London, profoundly humanitarian. Not for nothing was Battie's *Treatise on Madness* (1758) an attack (promptly repelled) against the therapeutic nihilism of the Monro family, who had owned and run Bedlam hospital for two centuries. Furthermore, by stressing insanity as alienation, as shown in the very title of his *Traité médico-philosophique sur l'aliénation mentale ou la manie* (1801), Pinel relocated madness *within man*, whether mind or body. But in so doing he gave pride of place not to insanity-as-illness (Foucault's *bête noire*) but to insanity as case history. Now this focus on the individual (a harbinger of Freud) was patently a remarkably progressive step – parallel, in fact, to a similar move in contemporary physical medicine which, as we shall presently see, was to be brilliantly chronicled by Foucault in his next book. Doerner can only conclude that Foucault, for all his authoring 'the first important approach' to the sociology of psychiatry, offers 'too one-sided' an account – one where the dialectics of the Enlightenment is 'unilaterally resolved in terms of its destructive aspect'.

In *The Birth of the Clinic: an Archaeology of Medical Perception* (1963) Foucault scrutinized a much shorter span, the rich history of medicine between the last third of the eighteenth century and the French Restoration (1815–30). Concentrating on old medical treatises, of which we are given fascinating interpretations, the book, which was commissioned by Canguilhem, unearths different 'perceptual structures' underpinning three successive kinds of medical theory and practice.

Two major shifts stand out. In the first, a 'medicine of species', still reigning around 1770, gave way to the first stage of *clinical* medicine. The medicine of species did in nosology what Linnaeus did in botany: it classified diseases as species. It was assumed that diseases were entities with no necessary connection to the body. Transmission of diseases occurred when some of their 'qualities', through 'sympathy', intermingled with the patient's kind of temperament (one was still close to Galen and his humoral views). 'Unnatural environments' were thought to favour the spread of disease, so that peasants were deemed to suffer from fewer illnesses than the urban classes (epidemics, unlike diseases, were not considered fixed entities but products of climate, famine and other external factors). By contrast, early clinical medicine was a 'medicine of symptoms': it regarded diseases as dynamic phenomena. Instead of being fixed entities, diseases were thought of as mixtures of symptoms. Symptoms, in their turn, were taken for signs of pathological developments. Consequently, in medical theory, the taxonomic charts of classical medicine were replaced by temporal continua, allowing in particular for an increased study of cases.

Finally, on the threshold of the nineteenth century, there emerged another medical paradigm: the clinical mind replaced the medicine of symptoms by a 'medicine of tissues' – anatomo-clinical theory. Diseases no longer denoted species or sets of symptoms. Rather, they now pointed to lesions in specific tissues. Physicians came to focus much more – in their attempt to gain pathological knowledge – on the individual patient. The medical *gaze* turned into a *glance*, a visual equivalent of *touch*, as doctors looked for hidden causes instead of just surface symptoms. Death – seen as a life process – became the great master of clinical anatomy, revealing through the decomposition of bodies the invisible truths sought by medical science.

Death and the individual, shows Foucault – the very themes of high romantic art and literature – were also underlying the new 'perceptual code' of medicine – a code which found its gospel in the *General Anatomy* (1801) of Xavier Bichat (1771–1801). As François Broussais (1772–1838; *Examination of Medical Doctrines*, 1816), building on Bichat's histology, based medical knowledge on physiology rather than simply on anatomy and explained fevers as pathological reactions due to tissue damage, the wheel came full circle: classical medicine died at the hands of scientific doctors. Classical medicine had an object – disease – and an aim – health. Clinical medicine come of age substituted the sick body for the disease as an object of medical perception, and normalcy for health as the desideratum of the healer's art. Thus the ideal of normalcy, debunked as a repressive prop in *Madness and Civilization*, turns up again under Foucault's hostile eye at the end of his history of the birth of modern medicine.

This time, however, the picture is much less burdened by anti-modern and anti-bourgeois prejudice. In his first, slender book, *Mental Illness and Psychology* (1954), Foucault had often reasoned as a 'cultural school' psychoanalyst, attributing mental disturbance to conflict-ridden capitalist society. In *Madness and Civilization*, more daringly, he stood on the side of (mythical) folly against bourgeois reason. Though he would probably acknowledge neither, one might say that he moved from the position of an Erich Fromm into that of a Norman Brown – from an emphasis on social blockage of human bliss to a call for the liberation of the Dionysian id. In *The Birth of the Clinic* no such outbursts are discernible. The book is very well written – indeed, composed with great literary skill – but its tone is not that far from the sober elegance of Canguilhem's own papers on the history of scientific ideas.

What *The Birth of the Clinic* did was to bring Foucault nearer to structuralism. An essay which speaks of perceptual codes and structures, describes the 'spatializations of the pathological', and insists on a non-linear rendering of intellectual history – on 'archaeology' as a Kuhn-like caesural account of paradigm shifts in medical thought – was bound to be compared to the theoretical idiom then in ascendancy in France. An able commentator, Pamela Major-Poetzl, rightly noticed that whereas *Madness and Civilization* tried to change our standard perception of madness but not our conventional way of thinking about history, *The Birth of the Clinic* does precisely the latter:[16] it introduces several *spatial* concepts dear to the structuralist mind.

Last, it should be noticed that *The Birth of the Clinic* also inaugurates, in Foucault's work, the problematic of the mode of *social insertion of discourses*. He grants a fair degree of autonomy in discourse-formation. However, this is not the whole story. He also wants to inquire into the concrete way a given discourse (e.g., medical thought) gets *articulated* with other social practices, external to it. At the same time, he tries hard to avoid coarse deterministic clichés like the omnibus base/superstructure 'explanations' in (vulgar) Marxism, and he strives to envisage more flexible patterns of explanation without falling into the cloudy abstractions common in the structural Marxism of Althusser and his followers, who talk a lot about 'overdetermination', 'structural causation' and 'structural effect' but seldom, if ever, come to grips with any empirical stuff (they don't like to dirty their hands with the analysis of real history).

The Birth of the Clinic contains chapters on the social context of big changes in medical theory and practice. For instance, we are shown how the government throughout the French Revolution, under duress because of the increase in the sick population in wartime, compensated for the lack of hospitals and competent physicians by reluctantly opening clinics. The clinic, in turn, made it possible to circumvent the medical guilds and their traditional lore, thereby helping to launch new 'perceptual structures' in medicine. Thus we can see that the causal relation between social context and paradigm shift in medical discourse is of indirect, even oblique, character. It is all a question of showing 'how medical discourse as a practice concerned with a particular field of objects, finding itself in the hands of a certain number of statutorily designated individuals and having certain functions to exercise in society, is articulated on practices that are external to it and which are not themselves of a discursive order.'[17] 'Articulated': here is the strategic word. As Roland Barthes liked to say, structuralism is very fond of 'arthrologies' – of reasoned disquisitions on links and connections.

3. An archaeology of the human sciences

The title of this section is literally the subtitle of Foucault's masterpiece, *Les Mots et les choses* (*The Order of Things* in English). Surprisingly, however, the book does not resume the problem of articulation of social and intellectual practices. Rather, it rejoices in an exuberant, insightful description of the latter. Foucault simply takes the Western discourses on life, wealth and language in order to grasp the conceptual background against which, during the nineteenth century, arose the sciences of man. The time-span is roughly the same as in *Madness and Civilization*: from the Renaissance to the present, stretched to the contemporary so that a word can be said not only on Freud but also on phenomenology and structural anthropology.

The inspiration to write *The Order of Things*, Foucault says in his foreword, came to him as he read a short story by Borges in which the ironic Argentinian refers to 'a certain Chinese encyclopaedia' in which 'animals are divided into: (a) belonging to the Emperor, (b) embalmed, (c) tame, (d) sucking pigs, (e) sirens, (f) fabulous, (g) stray dogs, (h) included in the present classification, (i) frenzied, (j) innumerable, (k) drawn with a very fine camel-hair brush, (l) et cetera, (m) having just broken the water pitcher, (n) that from a long way off look like flies.' The ludicrous oddness of such classification suggests to Foucault, through 'the exotic charm of another system of thought', 'the limitation of our own'. In other words, Borges' imaginary encyclopaedia can be taken as a symbol of alien patterns of categorization; the fable points to incommensurable systems *of ordering things*. The question, then, naturally arises: what are the borders of our own way of thinking? How do we, modern Westerners, order phenomena? Foucault's archaeology of the human sciences is an attempt to give an answer, presented in historical perspective, to such a question. The subject matter of his book are *fundamental cultural codes* imposing order upon experience.

Foucault picked up the label 'archaeology' to denote 'the history of that which renders necessary a certain form of thought'. 'Archaeology' deals with necessary, unconscious and anonymous forms of thought, which Foucault calls 'epistemes'. An episteme is the 'historical *a priori*' which, 'in a given period, delimits in the totality of experience a field of knowledge, defines the mode of being of the objects that appear in that field, provides man's everyday perception with theoretical powers, and defines the conditions in which he can sustain a discourse about things that is recognized to be true'.[1] Since epistemes are conceptual strata underpinning various fields of knowledge and corresponding to different epochs in Western thought, historical analysis must 'unearth' them – hence the archaeological model.

In the foreword to the English translation of *Les Mots et les choses*, Foucault describes thought-archaeology as a history of systems of 'non-formal knowledge'. The history of science, he tells us, has long favoured 'noble sciences' of the necessary such as mathematics and physics. Disciplines studying living beings, languages or economic facts, on the other hand, were considered too empirical and too exposed to external constraints 'for it to be supposed that their history could be anything other than irregular'. Foucault intends to redress the balance.

His focus will fall on three 'empiricities': life, labour, and language, or, more exactly, man as a living, a productive and a speaking animal, or again, man in his biological, his socio-economic and his cultural dimension. Natural history and biology, economics, grammar and philology will be his hunting grounds in *The Order of Things*. And – most important – Foucault is convinced that, *at a deep level*, there is a high degree of isomorphism between all these areas of knowledge, *within each epistemic phase*.

One might say, taking advantage of the renown of the Kuhnian concept, that Foucault wants to identify some scientific *paradigms*. But his paradigms are different from Kuhn's in three important ways. First, instead of referring to physics, they straddle, as we have just seen, one natural science (biology) and two social sciences (economics and linguistics). Secondly, they do not normally correspond to conscious principles, like those expounded by Newton, providing a model for scientific activity by specifying problems and setting up methods for their solution; rather, they are located beneath the level of conscious theorizing and methodological awareness. Kuhn's paradigms are 'exemplars' : they operate as concrete models shared by researchers in their scientific practice – a practice aimed at 'refining the paradigm'. As such, and insofar as they are 'more than theory but less than a world view', his paradigms are largely open-ended, implicit and even half-conscious – but they are not *by definition unknown to scientists* as Foucault's epistemes are. Foucault's conceptual grids are always out of reach for those whose thinking is bound by their laws.

Lastly, and precisely because they belong more to practice than to a scientific collective unconscious, paradigms are not – as stressed by Kuhn himself – strictly rule-bound; but epistemes definitely are:[2] they are 'fundamental codes', generative grammars of cognitive language. Ultimately the two concepts designate two basically different levels: paradigms may be 'more than theories' but, compared to epistemes, they surely are on the level of theories; epistemes, on the other hand, are more than world views – they are built in a still deeper layer of (un)consciousness.

Yet Foucault's *epistemes* are similar to Kuhnian paradigms in two other respects: (a) they are (to use Kuhn's own famous word) 'incommensurable', i.e., radically divergent from each other; and (b) they do not perish in response to a compelling independent body of contrary evidence and argument, but rather – as in Kuhn's 'Gestalt switches' within the scientific community, equivalent to mass religious conversions resulting from mysterious alterations of social psychology – in response to cultural sea changes. And just as Kuhn has his 'scientific revolutions' preceded by periods of paradigm-crisis, so Foucault (albeit with far less emphasis) shows the shortcomings and fatigue of at least two epistemes: the 'classical' (seventeenth to eighteenth centuries) and the 'modern' (essentially last century's).

There is, nevertheless, a last, important difference: Kuhnian crises are times of fierce competition, as old and new paradigms fight each other in a true struggle for life; and although the final victory of one of them stems from extra-rational causes, this Darwinian picture of paradigm-struggle seems to harbour a residual homage to the objective, immanent logic of scientific argument. After all, nowhere does Kuhn contend that, in the perpetual problem-solving which is science, once a solution to a particular puzzle is found under an old paradigm, it becomes ruled out under the new one.[3] This may sound inconsistent with his glaring rejection of a cumulative view of the history of science; but perhaps it is the latter which is inconsistent in itself. In any event, the evolution of Kuhn's thought, as shown in his famous Postscript to the second edition of *The Structure of Scientific Revolutions* (1970), went clearly towards the acknowledgement of a core of objectivity; he has come to recognize, or rather, to stress, in the words of David Papineau, 'the possibility that there are after all certain impartial bases of comparison with respect to which some theories can be shown to be objectively better than others'.[4] Foucault, by contrast, never grants as much. As a matter of fact, all his work since *The Order of Things* has moved far away from any such admission: 'objective knowledge' remained to him a foreign notion through and through.

An *episteme*, therefore, may be called a paradigm, providing it is not conceived of as an exemplar, a model of cognitive work. It is a basement (*sous-sol*) of thought, a mental infrastructure underlying all strands of the knowledge (on man) at a given age, a conceptual 'grid' (*grille*, in Foucault's Lévi-Straussian wording) that amounts to an 'historical *a priori*' – almost a historicized form of Kant's categories. Now such historical *a prioris* are not only incompatible but incommensurable: thus Buffon, as a true specimen of the classical episteme in the eighteenth century, was simply unable to see the point of the Renaissance naturalist Aldrovandi's fanciful history of serpents and dragons. Buffon's perplexity, says Foucault, was not due to the fact that he was less credulous or more rational a mind; rather, it was a consequence of the fact that his eyes were not linked to things in the same way as Aldrovandi's were *because they did not share the same episteme* (ch.II,4).

Foucault's history of epistemes – not to be confused, he warns, with the history of science or even a more general history of ideas – constantly underscores *discontinuities* between its historical blocks. We are given no systems of knowledge marching to a more faithful rendering, a more realistic grasp of a constant, stable object. Instead, all we get are 'enigmatic discontinuities' (ch.VII,1) between four epistemes: the pre-classical, up to the middle of the seventeenth century; the 'classical', up to the end of the eighteenth century; the 'modern'; and a truly contemporary age, which has only taken form since around 1950. The first and the last epistemes are barely sketched in *The Order of Things*: only the classical and the modern ages are fully described. And description, not causal explanation, of their sequence is all that interests Foucault; as he candidly states in his foreword, he deliberately brushed aside the problem of the causes of the epistemic change.

Although, as just recalled, Foucault's enterprise is no history of science, he had of necessity to rely on such a discipline in order to identify and organize his material. Actually, he gladly refers to a specific tradition within modern history (and philosophy) of science: the school of Bachelard, Cavaillès and Canguilhem, devoted to the history of *concepts*. Canguilhem is himself a pupil and successor (at the Sorbonne) of Gaston Bachelard (1884-1962), France's outstanding epistemologist in the thirties and forties. To a certain extent, Bachelard means to Foucault what Mauss meant to Lévi-Strauss and Blanchot to Barthes: a highly seminal protostructuralist approach to the conceptualization of their respective problems.

Bachelard gave pride of place, in his search for conceptual descents, to *discontinuities*. All his life he thundered against 'false continuities' assumed between ideas which were worlds apart in their historical intellectual contexts. In his *La Formation de l'esprit scientifique* (1936) he avoided a triumphalist, linear view of scientific progress by emphasizing the importance of 'epistemological obstacles'. In *Le Rationalisme appliqué* (1949) Bachelard brought into play the concept of *problématique*: a 'problematic' develops within a science under way, never from an intellectual and cognitive void. Therefore it connotes, not truth or experience in general, but always particular objects in a specific scientific domain, contemplated in its cognitive dynamic. Together with the sense of discontinuity – what we may choose to call the '*caesural*' view of scientific development – the notion of problematic was the second main bequest of Bachelard to Canguilhem, Althusser, and, through them, to Foucault. A third legacy, however, was no less significant: the strong *anti-empiricist* leanings of Bachelard's epistemology. Bachelard kept scientific reason and common sense firmly separated. 'Science is not the pleonasm of experience,' he wrote.[5]

Along with anti-empiricism went a solid distrust of Platonic theories of truth. Bachelard had learned from Léon Brunschvicg, the great Sorbonne epistemologist during the Belle Epoque, to recognize no prior truth: science is by no means a reflection of truth; just as work is an *antiphysis*, scientific work is an 'antilogy', a refusal of usual concepts. Scientists are 'the workers of evidence', which means they work, first and foremost, *on* the evidence. Science advances through the *cogitamus* of a scientific community for whom truth lies not in the given but in the *constructed*: scientific rationalism rests on a co-rationalism – of which, however, even in the sympathetic opinion of Canguilhem, Bachelard gave too psychologistic an account.[6]

Three, then, were the main legacies of Bachelard to structuralist epistemology: (a) caesuralism (the theme of the break or *coupure épistémologique*' ('*rupture*' in Bachelard), central in Foucault and Althusser; (b) anti-empiricism; (c) a *constructivist* view of science to which belong the concepts of 'problematic' and the virtual collapsing of rationality as such into mere scientific 'practice'. Moreover, from the outset he strove to free epistemology from the spell of Descartes. Where Descartes *reductively* equates science with *certainties* built on *simple objects*, Bachelard calls for an *induction* based on the *complex* data of open *objectifications* willingly contented with *probabilities*.[7] He also rejected the Cartesian idea of immutable scientific truths, progressively revealed to a system of knowledge that knows growth but not, in the main, structural change. This was too Platonic for Bachelard; he preferred to see Truth as an outcome of rational activity within the 'scientific city' (an echo of Georges Sorel,[8] who would in all likelihood have relished the phrase '*ouvriers de la preuve*' to describe scientists). Hyppolite wrote that Bachelard had the 'romanticism of intelligence'.[9] Indeed, his stress on risk and the fruitfulness of error does sometimes recall Sir Karl Popper's heroic view of science.

However, one thing is sure: Bachelard's anti-Cartesianism seems miles away from that of the structuralists. Bachelard was a rationalist who enthused about abstract thought and had no room for the structuralist love of intellectual *bricolage* and the 'logic of the concrete'. Again, he wrote a lot on caesuras and discontinuities, but didn't theorize about epochal blocks in the history of science. True, he warned there was no point in discussing alchemy and modern chemistry as though they belonged to the same conceptual universe – but he never spoke in similar terms of ages *within* modern i.e., Galilean, science. Significantly, when Kuhn's chronicle of paradigms in physics borrowed from French historians of science, it turned not to Bachelard but to Alexandre Koyré (1892–1964). Koyré was a Russian who studied under Husserl in Göttingen before moving into the circle of the anti-positivist rationalist, Emile Meyerson (1859–1933), in Paris. After the war Koyré spent regular spells at Princeton. The watertight contrast he drew between ancient and modern science as cultural worlds (*From the Closed World to the Infinite Universe*, 1957) – a tale of radically diverse scientific *Weltanschauungen* in different ages – cleared the ground for Kuhn's paradigm theory.

Koyré crucially anticipates both Kuhn and Foucault in that he stressed the role of 'extralogical factors' in the acceptance or rejection of scientific theories. Against positivist views, he insisted that the 'technical' value of a theory – its explanatory power – was by no means always the key to its victory in the history of scientific thought.[10] Koyré had been too much under the spell of Husserl: he knew that beneath scientific concepts there is a *Lebenswelt*, a lifeworld, saddled with a heavy 'philosophical infrastructure'. Foucault's eras of knowledge, the epistemes, are unconscious *Lebenswelten*. Foucault's job in *The Order of Things* consists in focusing on the *mutations* between epistemes. Mutation is a biological concept forged by Hugo de Vries (1848–1935) and rekindled in the work of François Jacob (*La Logique du vivant*, 1970),

Foucault's Nobel Prize-winning colleague at the Collège de France. In the Foucaldian idiom, a mutation occurs when one set of preconceptions (Koyré's philosophical infrastructure) gives way to another.

But in Foucault, epistemic mutations are fundamentally arbitrary. Epistemes succeed one another without any inner logic. Moreover they tend to constitute radically heterogeneous blocks of knowledge: absolute discontinuity is the supreme interepistemic law. Koyré, by contrast, allowed for some strategic common elements between distant epistemological ages, thereby making caesurae in the history of knowledge less absolute if not less sharp. In his view, the philosophical infrastructure of knowledge ages can *combine* what had been quite separate – even incompatible – before. A most impressive instance of this comes in his *Etudes d'histoire de la pensée scientifique* (1966), as he describes the philosophical ground of the rise of modern science in the mid-seventeenth century. Whereas many, like Whitehead, spoke of modern scientific thought as a revenge of Plato against the lord of medieval knowledge, Aristotle, Koyré depicted it as the product of an unholy alliance between Plato *and Democritus*: he correctly stressed the significance of the Democritean ontology of atom and void in the downfall of the Aristotelian notions of substance and attribute, potentiality and actuality. The revival of Democritus was what gave a thinker like Gassendi (who, unlike Galileo or Descartes, was no scientific inventor) such an important place in the theoretical grounding of modern science.[11] Now this combination of Platonic and Democritean elements was inconceivable to the ancient mind. Therefore, we have: (a) a caesural, i.e., non-linear or simply cumulative, conception of history, and (b) an admission of only *relative* heterogeneity between eras, due to the fact that the peculiarity of a new knowledge age can consist in its capacity to articulate prior elements originally quite alien to each other.

4. From the prose of the world to the death of man

Let us now turn, then, to the epistemes themselves. The oldest of them, irretrievably lost to our habits of mind, is the Renaissance paradigm. Foucault portrays it as 'the prose of the world', defined by the unity of words and things, *les mots et les choses*, in a seamless web of *resemblances*. Renaissance man, for Foucault, thought in terms of similitudes. There were four ranges of *resemblance: convenientia* connected things near to one another, e.g., animal and plant, earth and sea, body and soul, adding up to a 'great chain of being' (a topos classically studied by the master historian of ideas, Arthur Lovejoy). *Aemulatio* meant similitude within distance: thus the sky was said to resemble the face because it, too, has two eyes, the sun and the moon. *Analogy* had a still wider range, based less on similar things than on similar relations. Finally, *sympathy* likened almost anything to anything else, in virtually boundless identification: through it, each bit of reality was seen as drawn to another, all differences being dissolved in the play of such universal attraction. Sympathy linked, in particular, the fate of men to the course of planets, the cosmos to our humours. Its power was deemed so great that, left to itself, it would surrender the whole world to the sway of the Same. Fortunately, sympathy was moderated by its contrary, antipathy. The alternation between them set the pace to all resemblances.

Take, for example, the four elements: fire is hot and dry, hence it holds in antipathy water, which is cool and wet. The same applies to air (hot and wet) and earth (cold and dry) – again, antipathy rules. Therefore air is nicely put between fire and water, and water between earth and air: for in as much as air is hot, it is a good neighbour of fire; and insofar as it is wet, it goes along with water. ... Water's humidity, itself tempered by the air's warmth, mitigates the cold dryness of the earth; and so on and so forth.

You might think you are reading a page or two of Lévi-Strauss's *Mythologiques*, the most systematic modern scanning of hundreds of *coincidentiae oppositorum*. But in fact this comes straight from some contemporary annotations to a Renaissance book called *Le Grand miroir du monde*. Foucault quotes from a dozen quaint and curious tomes of forgotten lore: Ulisse Aldrovandi's *History of Monsters* (above, p. 38); Cesalpinus's *On Plants*; the philosophical disquisitions of Tommaso Campanella; the grammar of Petrus Ramus; Giambattista della Porta's *Natural Magic* and Blaise de Vigenère's *Treatise of Ciphers*; Jerome Cardan's *On Subtlety*; the works of Paracelsus.... Except for Ramus, Campanella and Aureolus Theophrastus Bombastus von Hohenheim (1493–1541), who wisely adopted the less daunting, though not more modest, *nom de plume* of Paracelsus ('higher than high'), all these authors, who flourished roughly between c. 1520 and 1650, are now almost utterly unknown, indeed unread. Quoting from them (as earlier from the medical authorities of yore) rather than from Renaissance celebrities such as Leonardo, Erasmus, Rabelais or Montaigne lent Foucault's own text an aura of erudition which, for many readers, veiled one of the main weaknesses in his scholarship: the often noticed fact that he was not conversant with the rich scholarly literature on these subjects.

Indeed, even his first historical master concept – resemblance – is not without some modern pedigree. Heidegger, for one, in a lecture first published in 1950 and translated into French in 1962,[1] sketched an antithesis between *correspondence* (*Entsprechung*) as the law of pre-modern thought and *representation* as the norm of modern knowledge. Heidegger explicitly tied up 'correspondence' with the principle of analogy, then contrasted it with the objectifying, reductionist glance of the modern representation. Similar hints can be found in Wilhelm Dilthey's earlier characterization of the Renaissance mind as 'thinking through images', 'plastic thought' as opposed to the Occam's razor, the sharp abstract rationality of the children of Galileo and Descartes.[2] Thus the modern *substitution of analysis for analogy* as the *forma mentis* of knowledge was an established theme in intellectual history well before *The Order of Things*. But it is only fair to say that if Foucault was not the first to detect it, at least he was the first to dissect it.

The episteme of resemblance or correspondence had also a special kind of cognitive idiom: *signature*, the sign of all similitudes. Renaissance knowledge assumed that God had put a mark or signature on things (on everything) in order to spell out their mutual resemblances. Yet since God's signatures were, more often than not, hidden, knowledge was bound to be an exegesis of the arcane. In these circumstances, *eruditio* often verged on *divinatio*: knowing was guessing. At any rate, knowing was neither observing nor demonstrating but interpreting. Signatures, in turn, put signs themselves under the principle of universal correspondence. Renaissance semiotics followed the ternary regime of the sign first proposed by the Stoics: it comprehended a signifier and a signified linked by a 'conjuncture', i.e., a resemblance of some sort. As a result, signs were not considered arbitrary; nor was language, in the 'prose of the world', a transparent denotation. No wonder it required endless interpretations – the search for the primal meanings, the signatures of words before Babel....

All of a sudden, in the seventeenth century, this episteme of correspondence collapsed. Knowledge started working otherwise: 'The activity of the mind', writes Foucault, 'will no longer consist *in drawing things together*, in setting out on a quest for everything that might reveal some sort of kinship, attraction, or secretly shared nature within them, but, on the contrary, in *discriminating*, that is, establishing their identities.'[3]

In other words, enter analysis, exit analogy. And this search for a stable, separate identity of things is what Foucault, just as Heidegger did before him, dubs (since the very title of his third chapter) *representation*. The rise of representation over the ruins of resemblance is the first epistemic mutation described in *The Order of Things*. It was all, curiously enough, heralded by a literary masterpiece, Cervantes' *Don Quixote*. Like a madman, Cervantes' knight is 'alienated in analogy'; and *Don Quixote* ushers in the new episteme because in the novel a ruthless reason based on identities and differences mocks over and again the very stuff of Renaissance knowledge: signs and similitudes.

Representation, therefore, was the soul of the *classical episteme* – roughly, the ground of knowledge between the mid-seventeenth century and the end of the eighteenth century. Its main structures were *mathesis*, a 'universal science of measurement and order', and *taxinomia*, the principle of classification, of ordered tabulation, best exemplified by Linnaeus' botany. Under mathesis and taxinomia, algebra and nomenclature, knowledge sought to replace infinite resemblance by finite differences, as well as the conjectural by the certain.[4] Furthermore, mathesis tended to exclude *genesis*: the knowledge of order was used to hold history in abeyance. At most, all that classical thought was able to do with history was to think of *ideal* geneses – Utopias projected on to an idealized primeval past.

Not surprisingly, the cognitive idiom itself – the 'language' of knowledge – came to be seen in a different light. The classical episteme, codified in this respect in the *Logic* of Port-Royal (1662), conceived of signification as a *binary* regime: language being regarded as transparent, there was no longer any general assumption of hidden links (the former 'conjunctures'), and therefore no need – as a rule – for elaborate interpretation. 'Divinatio' was quickly dismissed from the sphere of legitimate knowledge. Signifier and signified were viewed as connected in an arbitrary, but also crystal-clear manner.

Foucault writes at much greater length on the classical episteme than on its predecessor. Now he devotes one entire chapter to each of his chosen knowledge areas: linguistics, natural history and economics, respectively covering language, life and labour. He examines a host of dusty old works in each of these fields, and once again denies towering figures their usual privileges. Descartes gets as many mentions as obscure grammarians; the natural history of Linnaeus and the economics of Adam Smith are treated on an equal footing with several authors far less well known today. This unconventional approach deserves commendation, for it enables the historian of thought to cast a fresh look at many a lost or buried connection.

Right at the beginning of his book, Foucault gives representation, the spirit of the classical episteme, a graphic emblem. He muses over one of the jewels of the Prado, Velásquez' *Maids of Honour* (Las

Meninas, 1656). Velásquez shows himself looking at the viewer and represents his true models – the king and queen of Spain – only indirectly, through a dim reflection on a mirror placed on the rear wall of the studio. The painting's title is ironical: its true subjects (who occupy our position as viewers) are concealed. Foucault takes this as the symbol of representation itself: a knowledge where the subject is kept at bay.

One of the summits of baroque art, Velásquez' oeuvre contains more than a single instance of such a displacement of nominal subject matter. For example, in the wonderful picture following *The Maids of Honour*, the Prado's *Tapestry Workers*, the mythological theme of Pallas and Arachne is pushed into the background, whereas all the foreground is superbly given to the pedestrian workshop of the weavers. Just as in *Las Meninas*, in *Las Hilanderas* a shadowed front leads the eye to a bright spot at the back of the picture – but in each case the source of light seems cherished for its own sake, not for that of the insubstantial figures who inhabit it (the gentleman at the rear door in *Las Meninas*, the god and his victim Arachne in *Las Hilanderas*). In both works, moreover, the upstaging of the noble subject signals the painter's relish for organizing space not just by perspective but by the scansion of sheets of light underscoring receding planes. This play of light, together with the multiple focuses of optical interest, runs against the normal centrality of the main figure or figure group, thus imparting the space a (typically baroque) dramatic quality not necessarily evinced by the painting's subject as such. Art historians agree that Velásquez started his career in Seville towards 1620 as a painter impressed by Caravaggio and Zurbarán, and therefore very fond of tactile values (powerfully rendered in two of his pictures now in Britain, *The Old Woman Cooking Eggs* at Edinburgh and *The Water-carrier of Seville* at Apsley House in London). Yet he eventually evolved a daring *painterly* style which made him the most 'modern', i.e., protoimpressionist, of baroque masters. Contemporaries like the poet Quevedo were quick to grasp the new role of *colourism* – a legacy of Renaissance Venetian art – in the hands of Philip IV's court painter. A turning point in such evolution was reached with the ravishing *Toilet of Venus* (Rokeby

Venus, c. 1650) in the National Gallery, London – but *Las Meninas* and *Las Hilanderas* are widely regarded as the pictorial – and highly painterly – testament of Diego Velásquez.[5]

I have dwelt for a while on the aesthetic meaning of Velásquez' painting because it provides us with firm moorings if we are to embark on Foucault's far-flung metaphor of *The Maids of Honour* as an icon of the 'elision of the subject'. Luca Giordano, the virtuoso of the brush in the late baroque style, dubbed *Las Meninas* 'the theology of painting'.[6] In a sense, the saying seems to fit *Las Hilanderas* still better. Perhaps Pallas's scolding of poor Arachne, who is about to be turned into a spider, chastises the intellectual ambitions of painting, duly represented in the tapestry woven by Arachne, which reproduces no less than *The Rape Of Europe* of the greatest name in classical easel painting: Titian. In the foreground, on the other hand, Velásquez lovingly dresses in colour his humble carders and spinners, a plain reference to the no-nonsense of painting as craft....[7] *The Tapestry Workers* reads as a fable on human pride.

What about *The Maids of Honour*? Well, to begin with, the picture bore no such name in Velásquez' time. And its original title – 'The Family' – says much about the real meaning of its displaced subject. It is as though Velásquez had wished to pay a warm homage to his beloved sovereigns. At the centre of the stage, lit by her blonde hair and her magnificent silk garment, he put the Infanta Margarida Maria, first born of the king's second marriage. Halfway on the rear stairs, he painted the queen's tapestries steward, his own cousin Don José Velásquez. The whole scene bathes in a homely unsolemn mood, yet it does not lack gravity; the atmosphere breathes at once familiarity and demureness. The only playful episode – the gracious young dwarf gently kicking the dog (in the right-hand lower corner of the picture) – was actually an afterthought, for careful analysis has shown the dwarf's kicking leg to be an inspired pentimento, a subtle foil, as it were, to the pervasive self-restraint of the other characters. The court painter depicts himself in dignified modesty, working at a portrait of the royal couple. How could he represent also the latter, without detracting from their majesty? So he doesn't: he is content to associate his relative with his tribute and above all to give pride of place to the sovereigns' darling child, surrounded by her maids of honour, her duenna and her clowns. Did not Margarida Maria occupy, in the king's heart, the place once held by the lost Infante Baltasar Carlos, whom Velásquez so remarkably portrayed? Significantly, an elder infanta, Maria Teresa, born of the king's first wedlock, and future wife of Louis XIV, is absent from the picture. It so happens that she was by then a stern critic of her father's politics. At any rate, Philip IV welcomed Velásquez' homage: he kept the painting in his bedroom. Years later, he had the red cross of the Order of Santiago, which he bestowed on Velásquez shortly before his death, painted upon the painter's breast.[8]

So the tale told by *Las Meninas* is not as much the concealment of a subject as the respect for it. To Foucault, however, the painting encapsulates 'the representation of classical representation',[9] an epistemic system where that around which representation revolves must of necessity remain invisible. Velásquez, the Infanta and her party are all intent on staring at the king and queen – and they at them. The King only appears in the mirror insofar as he does not belong to the picture. Their gazes are reciprocal, their status unequal. The royal couple is the object (subject) of representation, yet they cannot (in the painting's circumstance) be represented themselves....

There would be no thick mystery had Foucault accepted, as does art history, that ultimately *Las Meninas* is Velásquez' *self*-portrait, painted in reverence for the king. It is therefore obvious that, for all the brilliance of his long comments on the picture – a charming portico to the elegant conceptual building of *The Order of Things* – Foucault is not at the bottom 'reading' *The Maids of Honour*; rather, he is reading *into* it a major postulate of his book's theory. Which postulate? The axiom that, in the classical episteme, the subject is bound to escape its own representation.

It all becomes much clearer if one bears in mind what happened, according to Foucault, in the next mutation – the demise of the classical episteme. By 1800, indeed, there happened 'a mutation of Order into History', things 'escaped from the space of the table'[10] and presented knowledge with 'internal spaces' that could not be represented in the classical sense of measurement and taxonomy.

Underneath the discontinuities of Linnaeus's *Taxinomia Universalis*, for example, a new concept of life crept in, refractory to natural history's tabulations, asserting an uncanny continuity between organisms and their environments. Natural history – a code of knowledge with no room for a history of nature[11] – gave way to biology. Meanwhile, philology supplanted classical general grammar; language, no longer seen as a transparent representation of thought, was endowed with historical depth. As for economics, the analysis of exchange was replaced by another deeper phenomenon: production. In the process, eighteenth-century 'analysis of wealth' got replaced by political economy. Thus life, labour and language ceased to be regarded as attributes of a stable nature and came to be envisaged as domains with a historicity of their own. History, the new goddess of knowledge, 'progressively imposed its laws' on 'the analysis of production, the analysis of organically structured beings, and, lastly, on the analysis of linguistic groups. History gives place to analogical organic structures, just as Order opened the way to successive identities and differences.'[12]

It is important to note that all the three classical disciplines share with their successors, biology, political economy and historic philology, is the bare outline of three empiricities – life, labour and language – as areas rather than objects: for the new sciences do by no means continue their archaic sisters, which are more displaced than truly replaced. Says Foucault: 'Philology, biology, and political economy were established, not in the places occupied by *general grammar*, *natural history* and the *analysis of wealth*, but in an area where those forms of knowledge did not exist, in the space they left blank, in the deep gaps that separated their broad theoretical segments and that were filled with the murmur of the ontological continuum.'[13]

Nobody knows for sure what is the murmur of an ontological continuum, but never mind: the message is clear enough. What Foucault is at pains to bring home, in his caesural fervour, is that there can be no bridge between any given epistemes. Whatever continuity can obtain is, of course, *inside* epistemes. Thus one may detect a certain degree of cumulative growth within the post-classical, or *modern*, episteme, to which Foucault devotes three of the last among the ten chapters of *The Order of Things*. In a first phase, stretching from about 1775 to the threshold of the nineteenth century, authors started to historicize life, labour and language, yet they still tried to handle these new empiricities with the conceptual weaponry of classical representations. Lamarck's way of regarding changing organic structures, Adam Smith's concept of labour, and William Jones's ideas on varying linguistic roots amounted to such a fragile compromise. Then, from around 1795 to circa 1825, a full-blooded modern episteme established itself. With Cuvier in biology, Ricardo in economics and Bopp in philology, the *forma mentis* of classical knowledge burst apart. In biological thought, function overcame structure. The study of language fastened to a welter of evolving roots. In economics, the circulation of goods came to be explained as a visible outcome of protracted processes of production. Everywhere, deeper, darker, denser forces were substituted for the surface regularities of classical knowledge; throughout different disciplines, modern thought imposed dynamic, historical categories of explanation.

Now Foucault's main point is that in all this *man* – the (main) subject matter of these three scientific discourses – got recognized in his factual, contingent existence. While the classical episteme was 'articulated along lines that [did] not isolate, in any way, a specific domain proper to man',[14] the categories of the modern episteme were all profoundly anthropological: ultimately, they all hinged on an 'analytic of [human] finitude'. Foucault invites us to awake from the 'anthropological slumber' which is the oxygen of modern knowledge. For we are haunted by history and humanism; and we are a prey to history as a form of thinking because of our humanist obsession – our man-besotted way of looking at reality. If under classical episteme man as the central subject of knowledge was – as the royal model in *Las Meninas* – missing, the modern episteme did more than redress the balance: it overdid it, by forgetting that man, as a fulcrum of knowledge through his personal or his collective finitude, is but a passing figure in the inscrutable pageant of epistemes:

As the archaeology of our thought easily shows, man is an invention of recent date. And perhaps one nearing its end. If those arrangements were to disappear as they appeared, if some event of which we can at the moment do no more than sense the possibility – without knowing either what its form will be or what it promises – were to cause them to crumble as the ground of Classical thought did, at the end of the eighteenth century, then one can certainly wager that man would be erased, like a face drawn in sand at the edge of the sea.[15]

These ominous sentences constitute the very last lines of *The Order of Things*. Now this was not exactly the first time structuralism gently denounced the human point of view in knowledge. Had not Lévi-Strauss calmly proposed the dissolution of man as a goal of human science? Nevertheless, in spite of some common overtones, our two thinkers are not saying the same thing. Whereas Lévi-Strauss uttered a wish in the name of science, what Foucault, at his most cryptic, did was something quite different: he hinted at a prospect which is rather like a *fate* in knowledge. When the tide of the next episteme comes, man as a space of knowledge will be washed away. What is the meaning of such an odd oracle?

Let us briefly recapitulate. The modern episteme, the episteme of history rather than order, unfolds itself as an analytic of man's finitude. Man is a being such that it is in him – through him – that we realize what makes knowledge possible. No doubt, grants Foucault, human nature was already playing a similar role in the eighteenth century. However, at the time, what empiricists such as Condillac focused upon were just the properties of representation – the mind's faculties – which enabled knowledge to get on its way: self-consciousness, memory, imagination. For an analysis of *concrete man*, as the subject matter of post-classical knowledge, this was not enough. Instead of an abstract 'human nature', a central place was given to man as a 'thick reality' and as such, a 'difficult object'[16] – nothing easily caught into the transparence of static representations, in the crystalline episteme of order and its clear-cut tabular trees. An analytic of finitude required that the preconditions of knowing be clarified by means of the very empirical contents given in human life: man's body, his social relations, his norms and values.

Now this put man, epistemologically speaking, in an awkward position. For, on the one hand, to know man boiled down to grasping the determinations of concrete human existence in the facts of life, labour and language, all of which mould man even before his birth as an individual. But on the other hand, research on both the physiological nature and the social history of knowledge, intent on laying bare the empirical contents of man's saga on earth, could not help presupposing a certain level of *transcendental* reason, since, in order to sever truth from error, science from ideology, knowledge needs a critical standard of some external bearing. As a consequence, man – the fulcrum of knowledge in the modern episteme – is bound to be 'a strange empirico-transcendental doublet' – an epistemological requirement almost impossible to meet in a satisfactory way. No wonder, then, such an ambiguous figure of knowledge[17] is threatened by the prospect of dissolution.

Foucault's reflections on this topic, vital as it is in the economy of *The Order of Things*, are terribly compressed. What exactly does he mean by the ambiguity (his own term) of the human doublet? Whatever it may be, it is emphatically a strictly epistemological puzzle. No room here for Pascal's half-angel, half-beast, or Kant's duality of moral freedom and natural determinism. What Foucault seems to have in mind is the phenomenological enterprise. Phenomenology, he claims, vows to grasp at once the empirical and the transcendental – for such is the goal of its programme, the analysis of the lived experience (Erlebnis,vécu). The phenomenologist focuses on experience because lived experience is at the same time the space where all empirical contents are given to consciousness and the original matrix which makes them meaningful. Phenomenology, adds Foucault, devised a 'mixed discourse' in a last-ditch attempt to solve the empirico-transcendental problem. But the attempt misfired, since phenomenologists did not face the real issue: does man (epistemologically speaking) really exist?

As to the 'doublet' problem itself, Foucault does not elaborate on it – which is all the more unfortunate, since this may be reckoned the philosophical heart of *The Order of Things*, the seat of its main argument against the heritage of modern knowledge. Instead, he just acknowledges its puzzling 'obscurity' and, leaving it at that, chooses to allude, in the same short section of the book, to a related but patently distinct dilemma: the swing, in modern knowledge, between 'positivism' (the reduction of man's truth to the empirical) and 'eschatology' (the anticipation of truth in a discourse of promise). Positivism and eschatology are said to be 'archaeologically inextricable'. Their oscillation, most conspicuous in thinkers like Comte and Marx, is, in Foucault's view, bound to occur at the core of knowledge so long as the modern, *anthropological* episteme prevails. Yet it is a sure sign of 'precritical naiveté' in modern thought – a theoretical innocence that phenomenology dispelled only at the price of its own failure.

What about the *human sciences* proper in all this? Is not the book intended as an archaeology of them? In *The Order of Things*, the function of the human sciences is, to put it bluntly, to examine the *meaning* of man to himself. Biology, economics and philology scrutinize life, labour and language in themselves, not in what they represent for man. But psychology, sociology and the study of culture probe into the given modes of meaning of his processes and activities.[18]

Yet there is more to it.[19] The human sciences, dealing with human meanings, are constantly self-critical: no sooner do they take a set of meanings normally employed by man as a living, a productive or a speaking animal, than they treat it as the surface of some deeper sense. The human sciences thrive on the critique of human consciousness. Their truest function is demystifying. Their calling lies not in the increase of rigorous, precise knowledge (the human sciences are not sciences, says Foucault), but in the critical shuttle between consciousness and the unconscious: 'a human science exists, not wherever man is in question, but wherever there is analysis – within the dimension proper to the unconscious – of norms, rules, and signifying totalities which unveil to consciousness the conditions of its forms and contents.'[20]

The unconscious is crucially important to Foucault's theory of knowledge. The episteme of man is also the realm of his double: of the Other or the 'unthought' (*impensé*), Foucault's label for everything that falls outside man's self-representation at any given point in knowledge. To man, 'the Other' is 'not only a brother but a twin'; he is bound to him in an 'unavoidable duality'. Now there are some knowledges – psychoanalysis, ethnology – which specialize in keeping the self-critical thrust of the human sciences at its maximum power. They are 'counter-sciences' in hot pursuit of the Other, of the unthought, in sum: of the unconscious, be it in man (psychoanalysis) or culture (ethnology). And above or beyond these approaches to the unthought, there has now come of age a discipline offering a deciphering still more fundamental: structural linguistics. It is the third and strongest of the counter-sciences, because its object spreads all over the field of the human and also because it is the only one of the three susceptible of formalization.[21] By thus rescuing these counter-sciences from the discredited 'anthropological sleep' of modern knowledge, Foucault honoured the heartland of the 'structuralist revolution': the province of Saussure, Lévi-Strauss and Lacan.

The compliment was soon returned, at least by the younger wing of the structuralist brigade. Calling Foucault's archaeology a 'heterology', Michel Serres described it as an 'ethnology of European knowledge'.[22] A knowledge depicted as the very opposite of the Enlightenment's ideal: culture-bound instead of universal, epoch-relative instead of cumulative, and eroded, not by healthy doubt, but by the inhuman destructiveness of time. A knowledge where the human sciences are no science, and science itself possesses no logical stability, no lasting criteria of truth and validity. What *The Order of Things* proclaims is the eclipse of man as a ground of thought; what it achieves is a disturbing suggestion that knowledge itself may be no more than our persistent self-delusion.

5. The 'archaeology' appraised

Les Mots et les choses is a long, brilliantly written book full of valuable insights and raising a whole set of important issues of epistemology and the history of thought. Its philosophical prose, often too 'literary', is, however, strewn with gnomic utterances, tantalizing hints, and a taste for verbal drama rather than logical argument.[1] There is a façade of neatness, even a craze for symmetry ('the quadrilateral of language', 'the trilateral of knowledge', etc.), but the overall effect is far more florid; it reminds one of a master of an apocalyptic genre who sometimes indulged in writing *more geometrico*, a Spengler toying with the style of Spinoza. How are we to assess its views and above all its vision?

Foucault's project is to provide a historical account in depth of the emergence of the human sciences. As we saw, the book encapsulates a quest for the *'fundamental codes'* of our culture, which rule – states the preface – 'its language, its perceptual schemata, its exchanges, its technique, its values, the hierarchy of its practices'. It was of course his ambition to lay bare cultural codes by describing them in their forms and articulations, *regardless of their experimental referents in social and physical reality*, that put Foucault's archaeology, willy-nilly, in the company of structuralism, and led many to assimilate his enterprise to the theoretical model-making of Lévi-Strauss (the savage mind's widespread grids) or Barthes (the semiotic minicodes underpinning 'intransitive' literary meanings).

Yet all the historical digging was conducted for the sake of elucidating the predicament of *modern* knowledge. In this sense, *The Order of Things*, 'a partial exploration of a limited region' which, notwithstanding, forms, in his own words, together with *Madness and Civilization* and *The Birth of the Clinic*, the sketch of 'a set of *descriptive experiments*,[2] represents a first go at that critical history of the present that defines Foucault's overarching purpose as a philosopher for our times. The anatomy of epistemic mutations was a pre-condition of understanding the rise and fall of man as a mainstay of a certain historical kind of knowledge.

As *our* seismic change in thought-stratum gathers momentum, claims Foucault, contemporary knowledge will probably not only cease to be history-drunk – it will also get rid of its ingrained anthropocentricity. To be sure, 'humanists', including radicals with an archaic cognitive equipment, will protest both at such diagnosis and at such a prospect; but let them cry in vain. Archaeologists have no time for elegiac feelings – they must steel themselves to their harsh duties as *'primitifs d'un savoir nouveau'*. Such is, in broad outline, the message of vintage Foucault, 1966. Can we say of it – as has been said of the excellent, elegant Médocs and Pomerols of that same year – that it is at its peak by 1985?

The answer very much depends on what we get when we climb down from the vision to the prosaic but indispensable task of ascertaining the real value of its particular views. His placing of Marx close to Ricardo sounds quite convincing. Foucault's dictum that Marxism belongs in the nineteenth-century episteme 'as fish in water'[3] could stir up an outcry only in as Marxified an intellectual culture as the French in the sixties (Sartre: Marxism is 'the insurpassable philosophy of our time'); still, it hit the nail right on the head. Moreover, besides sharing with the pessimist Ricardo the historicization of the economy, by dint of categories such as scarcity and production as well as the labour theory of value, Marx the revolutionary shared also with his century, as we have seen, the unholy alliance between positivism and eschatology. There are worse ways of grasping the philosophical gist of Marxism.

Unfortunately most of Foucault's bold historical points are far from being so accurate. For example, he downplays the difference between rational thought and magic in the Renaissance. To him, Renaissance magic and humanist science were part and parcel of the same episteme – the rule of resemblance and signature. Yet, as experts on humanist magic are the first to admit, the language of signatures never encompassed all of Renaissance knowledge, not even – notes a critic – at that moment, in the late sixteenth century, when it was most written about.[4] Not only was the dominance of analogy over and above analysis not all-embracing but it often met staunch opposition. In France, for instance, there was during the Renaissance a dominant humanist tradition which scoffed at magic, Hermeticism, the farrago of Paracelsus's screeds, the claims of astrology, and the whole hotch-potch of 'signatures' and 'correspondences'. The literati of Montaigne's generation were a case in point: far from conflating erudition and the occult, they condemned 'divinatio' in the name of 'eruditio'. Montaigne himself derided astrological almanacs and the horoscope mentality (*Essais*, bk I, ch.XI, 'Des prognostications').[5] Nor of course was opposition confined to France: the founder of anatomy, Brussels-born and Padua-teaching Andreas Vesalius (1514-64), was equally adamant in his rejection of all doctrines of signatures.

Moreover, by insisting on an absolute caesura between Renaissance thought and the classical episteme since the mid-seventeenth century, Foucault makes almost unintelligible the evident and decisive continuity between the labours of Copernicus (a scientific innovator who was not above Hermetic beliefs) and the Kepler-Galileo line, which was the fountainhead of modern science. Yet continuity there was, regardless of the difference in their epistemic casts of mind. On the other hand, historians of science have stressed the importance of late fifteenth-century Florentine Neoplatonism for Copernicus' heliocentricity, Neoplatonism being at the time the normal carrier of the Hermetic and Cabalistic traditions of high magic and hylozoism – including the mystique of the sun. On the other hand, we have it on the unsuspected authority of the best interpreters of Renaissance Hermetic-Cabalist ideas that Copernicus reached his astronomical revolution (published in 1543, the same year as Vesalius' *De humani corporis fabrica*) by pure mathematic calculation, *unaided by magical belief*; and that a century later, Kepler – who still thought of his discovery about planetary orbits as a confirmation of the 'music of the spheres' – sharply distinguished between true mathematics and the Pythagorean or Hermetic mystical ways of dealing with numbers.[6]

Now if we put two and two together, we are bound to conclude that whether or not touched by beliefs germane to the analogical cast of mind, Renaissance scientists from Copernicus to Kepler achieved their epoch-making advances in substantial continuity with the Galilean mathematization of nature. In fact, the 'occult' went on acting as a nice occasional motivation for mathematical analysis until at least a century and a half after Kepler. As Richard Westfall has recently reminded us, Newton's long interest in alchemy taught him to consider ideas of action and force susceptible of mathematical treatment, as opposed to a mechanist description of the sky.[7] In sum, 'analysis' was not hampered – let alone swallowed up – by 'analogy'; and empirico-demonstrative knowledge found its own way without bondage to speculative 'interpretation'. The growth of mathematics in astronomy and physics was the royal path of such cognitive progress.

The trouble is that Foucault cares little (much less, for instance, than Koyré) for the mathematization of the world since the first steps of modern science. In his mathesis-cum-taxonomy picture of the classical episteme, it soon becomes obvious that tabulation rather than measurement is his pet idea. If Galileo, Descartes and Newton do not weigh very heavily in *The Order of Things*, it is not just owing to the anti-'heroic' parti-pris of the work – it is also because, in Foucault's view, mechanism and mathematics were not genuine, all pervasive epistemic structures.

In fact, however, if one is to believe classical accounts such as Whitehead's *Science and the Modern World*, mathematics was crucial in the rise and consolidation of modern science. The 'new' science stood on the side of Pythagoras and Plato against Aristotle, because Aristotle was the genius of taxonomy, and the advancement of knowledge needed something more than fine classifications; it needed the generalizing power given by number alone, and by that generalization of arithmetic itself which is algebra. The triumph of modern science was a revenge of Euclid and Archimedes on the long sway of Aristotelian physics. For centuries, learned circles thought that while the qualitative physics of Aristotle did 'explain' nature, mathematical theories (like Ptolemaic astronomy) merely 'saved the appearances'. Then came the Copernican revolution. In its wake, Galileo extolled Archimedes and criticized Aristotelian physics precisely for its non-mathematical character. Meanwhile the old controversy between mathematical theory and palaeophysics had already been settled, in favour of the former, by Kepler, an accomplished mathematician who assigned two goals to astronomy: to 'save the appearances' and '*to gaze at the structure of the universe*', that is to say, to explain nature.[8] The full title of Newton's magnum opus – 'Mathematical Principles *of Natural Philosophy*' – says it all.

True, in the areas scrutinized in *The Order of Things*, mechanism and mathematics were not in any sense prominent. They were irrelevant to grammar and philology and long absent from natural history and biology; as for mathematics in economics, not as sheer statistics but in a strong analytic capacity, it dates from a rather late theoretical formation in the modern episteme: the neoclassical school led by Jevons, Menger, Walras and Marshall, whose core – marginal utility theory – was first presented by Jevons in a paper read in Cambridge in 1862 under the title 'Notice of a general mathematical theory of political economy'.[9]

Natural history remained of course stubbornly taxonomic during the golden age of French mathematics – the age of Lagrange and Laplace, Monge and Carnot. But the point is, had Foucault the right – after so restricting the range of sciences under scrutiny – to present as *generally* valid an episteme whose description rested on such a narrowed basis of scientific record? At any rate one important question cannot be ignored: how was it that, throughout two centuries of sheer mathematical genius (from Descartes, Newton, Leibniz and the Bernoullis to Gauss, Boole, Riemann and Cantor) the unconscious ground of Western science was chiefly taxonomic? As Piaget has noticed, whilst taxonomy – the tabular episteme of Foucault's classical age – belongs rather low on the ladder of logical thought, Newtonian calculus presupposes a much higher degree of logical sophistication.[10] How can the self-same episteme support such different levels of thought? Even Canguilhem, ever friendly to Foucault's project, worried about the neglect of physics in the neat architecture of *The Order of Things* – and realized that a consideration of physics would undermine the crucial theory of strict caesuralism. Canguilhem's objection seems cogent enough: the sequence Galileo–Newton–Maxwell–Einstein does not offer breaks similar to those that can be found between, say, Buffon and Darwin. In other words, Newton is *not* refuted by Einstein, any more than Darwin is by Mendel. It follows that we can make little sense of the stark caesura inserted by Foucault between the classical and modern epistemes. In the actual history of science some classical discourses (e.g., Newton) have been integrated into the subsequent episteme; others (e.g., natural history) haven't. Nor can this difficulty for archaeology be disposed of by simply choosing to disregard it on the pretext that it belongs to another kind of study – the only excuse Foucault makes. I can't help sharing Canguilhem's doubt: is it really possible, in the case of *theoretical* knowledge in the scientific sense, to grasp its conceptual specifics *without reference to a norm*, that is, without taking into account its success or failure as scientific theory?

The problem would hardly have risen had Foucault not insisted that 'in any given culture and at any given moment, there is always *only one episteme* that defines the conditions of possibility of all knowledge'.[12] In other words, epistemes are monoliths – they are emphatically unitary blocks of knowledge. Accordingly, at each epistemic mutation things simply cease, all of a sudden, to be 'perceived, described, expressed, characterized, classified, and known in the same way' as before.[13] Again, in his preface he entreats us to regard the natural history of Linnaeus and Buffon as related, not to the later labours of Cuvier or Darwin, but to distinct yet contemporary fields like classical 'general grammar' or the analysis of wealth of Law and Turgot.... Compared to the 'massive changes' in epistemic structure at the close of the eighteenth century, says Foucault, the 'quasi-continuity' of ideas across the two ages is just a 'surface effect'.

True, in *The Archaeology of Knowledge* he warns that epistemes ought not be regarded as 'totalitarian', i.e., holistic concepts: the dominance of an episteme does not mean that every single mind thought along the same lines in a given age and culture. In *The Order of Things* he writes half-apologetically, 'the absence of methodological sign-posting may have given the impression that [...] analysis were being conducted in terms of cultural totality'[14] – but in fact an episteme is nothing of the sort.

However, his disclaimer is hardly satisfactory, for at least two reasons. First, it is difficult to see how the concept of episteme in *The Order of Things* could have been *misconstrued* as holist: it really is the actual text itself that makes it sound very much so – a text which, by the way, Foucault never cared to amend. Second, and more important, it could hardly be otherwise: for, if one starts granting epistemes too much flexibility and heterogeneity, if one makes them truly pluralistic, then what is gained in factual, historical accuracy is lost on the interpretive side, since eventually each episteme would scarcely qualify as a binding cognitive infrastructure.

Combined with his watertight view of epistemological breaks, Foucault's presentation of epistemes as monoliths forces his archaeology to ignore blatantly at least six kinds of phenomena.

First a portrait of epistemes as totally unconnected monoliths is bound to overlook *transepistemic* streams of thought. Yet if the epistemic approach refuses to take these phenomena into consideration, a serious problem is visited upon it. Its name is *anachronism*. And as a matter of fact, it appears that the more we stick to Foucault's periodization, the less his epistemes hold water: for in all of them there are 'anachronisms' galore. Let us just mention four glaring examples.

In the chapter on the Renaissance episteme, Foucault sets great store by the *Grammaire* of the humanist Petrus Ramus (Pierre de la Ramée), first published in 1572. Taking Ramus's work for a fine specimen of the analogic cast of mind of the episteme of correspondences, he contends that for Ramus the intrinsic 'properties' of letters, syllables and words were studied as uncanny marks of 'magic' forces like sympathy and antipathy. Now George Huppert, a professor at the University of Illinois and a member of the Chicago circle, has shown Ramus's *Grammar* to be 'a remarkably lucid work [...] not in the least tainted by hermetic philosophy or scholastic speculation about the quality of words'. Ramus's theory of language turns out to be quite empirical and rational: thus when he speaks of the 'properties' of words he just means what is conspicuously proper to them, as in the case of articles being put in front of nouns or pronouns, etc. Ironically, whereas the Cartesian Mersenne, writing half a century after Ramus, still asked himself, however reluctantly, whether there were occult correspondences between words and things, secret meanings known to Adam and lost since the Fall, Ramus had no truck with it: to him, words were just phonetic transcriptions; hence his proposals to drop dead letters like the g in 'ung' or the s in 'tesmoigner'.[15] Definitely – *pace* Foucault – no trace of magic interpretations, no taste for the occult.

Another signal case of Foucaldian misconstruction is the treatment of the Renaissance ornithologist, Pierre Belon, whose *History of the Nature of Birds* came out in 1555. Until *Les Mots et les choses*, everybody agreed to regard Belon's treatise – the work of a man who performed many dissections single handed besides naming 170 European bird species, thereby earning the admiration of later fellow naturalists – as a remarkable early example of comparative anatomy. Published in the decade following the great work of Vesalius, his *Histoire des oyseaux* contained, in text and plate, the first detailed comparison of the skeletons of man and bird. Foucault knows this but refuses to be taken in by the pious legends of the scientific progress ideology: with true *esprit de système*, he flatly decrees that for all its precision Belon's analysis can only read as comparative anatomy 'to an eye armed with nineteenth-century knowledge. It is merely that the grid through which we permit the figures of resemblance to enter our knowledge happens to coincide at this point (and almost no other) with that which the sixteenth century laid over things.'[16] Poor Buffon, who so often quotes Belon in his own *History of Birds* – maybe he didn't know how to tell a mere epistemic 'coincidence' from genuine comparative anatomy. Or is it rather – as Huppert argues[17] – that Belon was a superb observer, a keen taxonomist (he has even been credited with devising a Linnaeus-like binary nomenclature), an outstanding pioneer of natural history – so much so that denying his work a scientific purpose while assimilating it, on an 'archaeological level', to the fantastic teratology of Aldrovandi, is just silly?

Another anachronism in epistemic terms: Foucault speaks of

organic structure as a concept belonging to biological thought in the post-classical episteme. Not so, says Georges Sebastian Rousseau, the noted Pope scholar, author of *Organic Form: the Life of an Idea* (1972). If Foucault had read the modern scholarship on eighteenth-century naturalists (e.g., Philip Ritterbush's 1964 study), he would have realized that organic structure as a metaphysical assumption was by no means a novelty in Cuvier, but a concept with a long ancestry and in particular a rich history in the Age of Enlightenment.[18]

It seems that the rigidity of his arch-caesural notion of episteme made Foucault interpret quite wrongly figures and trends of thought as significant as Ramus, Belon and organicism. By contrast, in our final case of epistemic anachronism, also forcefully pointed out by G.S. Rousseau, the problem was not one of misunderstanding but of defective information. In *The Order of Things*, the works of Port-Royal logicians and grammarians are given pride of place in the description of the classical episteme. Indeed, the Port-Royal *Logic* (1662) enjoys a special status in Foucault's analysis, for it features as a curious instance of cognitive awareness among the normally unconscious epistemic rules. Thus the classical semiotic regime, which Foucault deems to be unconsciously at work in all other fields of classical knowledge, was actually stated by the Port-Royal logicians Arnauld and Nicole, not – as the other main coordinates of the classical episteme – *inferred* from classical discourse by Foucault. As for the Port-Royal *Grammaire générale et raisonnée* (1660), due to Arnauld and Lancelot, it is of course one of the purest samples of classical knowledge. Port-Royal grammatical thought, centred as it is on a theory of representation, is deemed by Foucault a gem of the episteme of order and clarity – a perfect pendant of Cartesian philosophy. Unfortunately, however, it so happens that the chief model of Port-Royal grammarians, according to Lancelot's own testimony, was not Descartes but a certain Sanctius. Now, Sanctius, alias Francisco Sánchez de las Brozas (1523–1601), published his *summa*, the one-thousand-page *Minerva, seu de causis linguae latinae* in 1585, that is, at the height of the vogue of the doctrine of signatures and the Hermetic literature.[19] Quite a puzzle for the neat table of Foucaldian epistemes: for the *Minerva* owes more to Quintilian than to any anticipation of modern philosophy; and yet it was Sanctius, not Descartes, whom Port-Royal grammar hailed as its main theoretical source; Sanctius and – others have pointed out – the elder Scaliger (Julius Caesar Scaliger) whose own grammatical work was published considerably earlier, in 1540.[20]

The second category of phenomena systematically neglected by Foucaldian archaeology are *epistemic lags*. Now the history of science is fraught with debates between tenants of backward views and pathbreakers and their followers; and more than once their clash opposed different epistemic casts of mind within the life-span alloted to an episteme by Foucault. Jan Miel has spotted a telling instance: the correspondence between Pascal and the Père Noël about the vacuum.[21] Father Noël had muddled thoughts on it, involving arbitrary comparisons and more generally a leaning towards analogical fireworks using 'animist' tenets like the doctrines of the four elements and humours. Pascal pleaded for a less equivocal use of terms and a less anthropomorphic view of nature, ruling out, in this juncture, the idea that nature so 'detests' vacuums that she just rushes to fill them. Pascal's strictures impeccably obey the analysis-rather-than-analogy approach typical of the classical episteme. To be sure, Pascal and the Père Noël were exchanging letters in 1647–48, when – according to Foucaldian chronology – the classical episteme was barely born. But if epistemes are monolithic blocks which come and go *all of a sudden* – if there is no epistemic vacuum – how can we account for the knowledge-structure lag embodied by the good Père?

We can give the third place among significant phenomena systematically overlooked by Foucaldian archaeology to the *return* of concepts or conceptual moulds long ousted by the evolution of thought and which, nonetheless, once returned, prove still capable of inspiring fruitful scientific research. My favourite candidate for an illustration is the notorious concept of phlogiston, known to everybody with a smattering of history of chemistry. The phlogiston, it may be remembered, was a hypothetical substance believed to dwell in all combustible bodies and to be released during their burning: it was 'the matter of fire'. This theory contained an assumption dating from Antiquity: the claim that, when anything burns, some of its substance disengaged from it, escaping in the flames and leaving the burnt body reduced to its original components. The Aristotelians thought that what was thus released was the 'element' fire. By 1670, a contemporary of Boyle, the German chemist, J.J. Becher, declared it to be oily, fatty earth (*terra pinguis*), thereby formulating the idea of the phlogiston as a substance. Then, over the first third of the eighteenth century, another German chemist, George Ernst Stahl, elaborating this view, coined the name phlogiston and gave the concept wide currency. By 1750, the doctrine of phlogiston was established in all Europe. In the last quarter of the century – the very time of the classical episteme's breakdown – it was to prove a formidable die-hard, the main target of the founder of chemistry, Lavoisier. Suffice it to recall that when Joseph Priestley, in the 1770s, managed to isolate oxygen by heating some oxides his explanation of this great feat (actually slightly anticipated by the Swede Carl Wilhelm Scheele) was still so couched in the old chemical persuasion that he called oxygen 'dephlogisticated air'.

Now it had long been known – e.g., to Boyle – that substances in the act of burning took something out of the air, increasing in weight as a result; and when, in the same years of Priestley's oxygen experiments, Lavoisier demonstrated that the increase in the weight of calcinated metals was due to their taking an 'elastic fluid' out of the air, the phlogiston dogma was mortally wounded. Lavoisier delivered his formal attack on it in 1783. In 1800, however, Priestley was still hitting back; in that year, he printed a *Doctrine of Phlogiston Established and the Composition of Water Refuted*.[22]

The point I am trying to make rests on two conclusions. First, the phlogiston idea, no matter how wrong an explanation, had an undeniable heuristic role. Indeed, it led to many experiments, amounted to the first fruitful generalization in chemistry and foreshadowed something like a true, 'problematic'. It has been said that from 1750 onwards there emerged a history of chemistry, whereas prior to the spread of phlogiston theory all that had existed was a history *of chemists* – each one with his own different views and problems, without a common Fragestellung, a shared visualization of the discipline's issues. Secondly, and notwithstanding all this heuristic value, belief in the phlogiston was clearly an odd Aristotelian ghost haunting European science when the classical episteme was in its full maturity. Significantly, its creator, Stahl, was also a vitalist biological theorist who practically revived Aristotle's concept of psyche.[23] In sum, the phlogiston marked a blatant 'return of the repressed' in terms of the evolution of scientific thought. But such an archaism was dialectically instrumental in the launching of chemistry as a science (to the point that Lavoisier himself used the phlogiston concept to describe his first experiments) and at any rate is quite unaccountable for within the archaeological framework of Foucault. If anything, the long life of the phlogiston theory seems easier to explain with the help of some *sociology* of science. Lavoisier's revolution was greeted by mathematicians and physicians but resented by most of his fellow chemists, who stuck to their Stahlian prejudices even when they were towering discoverers like Priestley. Craft, not episteme, sheds light on a scientific debate that Priestley himself – a skilful theologian to boot – deemed one of the hottest controversies in intellectual history. But again, no believer in epistemic monoliths could ever begin to understand the rise and fall of phlogiston.

Physics, mathematics and chemistry do seem to give the lie to Foucault's exaggerated caesuralism. They are modes of thought overarching three epistemes (mathematics) or staging their own breakthrough via a dialectical return of past forms of thought (chemistry). Transepistemic problematics, epistemic lags and dialectical returns are all phenomena alien – indeed, refractory – both to strict caesuralism and to the view that epistemes are compact, homogeneous conceptual infrastructures. In the main, however, they are *interepistemic* issues. Three further problems, on the other hand, fly more exclusively in the face of the second dogma – epistemes as monoliths. They cast doubt on the accuracy of Foucault's picture of *intraepistemic* realities.

The first of these problems refers to the fact that, *taken synchronically*, Foucault's epistemes – contrary to their allegedly massive unity – seem to encompass a lot of *heterogeneity*. We saw it in the case of magic and science, often magic-cum-science, during the

Renaissance, both in astronomy (Kepler) and natural history (Belon). We might add, borrowing a clever suggestion from Pierre Burgelin, [24] the case of nominalism in the dawn of the Renaissance era – a philosophical trend clearly bent on logic and abstraction, and as such difficult to harmonize with the '*pensée sauvage*' of Foucault's 'resemblance' episteme. Readers familiar with modern descriptions of the pluralism of Renaissance thought, such as those offered in the studies of Paul Oskar Kristeller, will not in the least be put off by the idea of such a coexistence (pacific or not) of pre-modern rationalisms, such as nominalist philosophy, and the more rhetorical than logical thought of the humanist movement. [25] Once again, the problem is largely inexistent - or rather, it exists only as a problem for the rigidity of Foucault's 'vertical history'. A third instance of intraepistemic difficulty, also first hinted at by Burgelin, [26] deals with one important development in the life sciences during the classical episteme: how far, in fact, can the episteme of tabular order described by Foucault accommodate the theories put forward by the so-called 'classical microscopists' in Bologna, London and the Netherlands within the second half of the seventeenth century? How did concepts like 'spontaneous generation' and the homunculus enter the otherwise powerful minds of Malpighi's and Hooke's generation – a group of first-rate observers who were born when Galileo and Descartes were publishing their main works? [27]

If epistemes are far more internally differentiated than the archeological gaze cares to acknowledge, it comes as no surprise to hear that, in the name of its unitary obsession, *The Order of Things* often overrates the position and prestige of some intellectual trends. Thus while, as we saw, Foucault erects the Port-Royal grammar into a theory of representation valid for all the classical age, Georges Gusdorf, in volume VI of his monumental *Les Sciences humaines et la conscience occidentale* – a work whose range of erudition dwarfs Foucault's – shows how the strong normative drive of the 'grammaire générale *et raisonnée*', aiming as it did at a logical streamlining of linguistic usage, was stubbornly resisted by a cultural institution as strategic as the French Academy. Is it not highly intriguing to see the Académie holding out against one of the prize areas of the episteme of order? Yet this was exactly what it did: from 1647 to 1704, it withstood every major attempt to harness its authority to convert the usage of French into a verbal French garden.[28] So the burden of proof in the idea that the classical mind had given itself entirely to the logicism of 'general grammar' rests indeed on Foucault's shoulders. If his epistemes do resemble monoliths, classical culture definitely didn't.

Finally, there are intraepistemic problems arising from a diachronic perspective. Two kinds come to mind almost at once. First, there may be *collapses* within an episteme. Thus, as the historian of grammar Jean-Claude Chevalier has shown, the Port-Royal grammar, the very jewel in the crown of Foucault's classical episteme, was badly misunderstood at the time of the *Encyclopédie*[29] – well before the next epistemic mutation according to Foucault.

Secondly, there may occur *intraepistemic breaks*. Jan Miel[30] pointed out a crucial instance of this: the momentous changes in the philosophical outlook and scientific thought towards the end of the *Grand Siècle*, as part and parcel of what long ago Paul Hazard, in a rather sensationalist vein, dubbed 'the crisis of European mind'.[31] This of course broaches the vast and thorny question of the general attitude of the *philosophes*, as heirs to Bayle and Locke and fans of Newton, towards seventeenth-century philosophy – a question the proper study of which, in the expert's view, has yet to be made.[32] We know the *philosophes*' dislike for the *esprit de système*. Since Ernest Cassirer's illuminating classic, *The Philosophy of the Enlightenment* (1932), we realize that the Enlightenment significantly changed the concept of reason. While, for Descartes, Spinoza or Leibniz, reason was 'the territory of eternal truths', the next century no longer saw reason as a treasure of principles and fixed truths, but simply as a faculty, the original power of the mind, to be grasped only in the exercise of its analytical functions.[33]

However, as Cassirer himself took pains to stress, it all amounted to a shift of emphasis rather than a different view of knowledge. To be sure, knowledge of particulars came to be more valued than knowledge of universals; the accent of knowing went *from 'principles' to 'phenomena'*. But the self-confidence of reason and the will to analysis were never threatened. Although it was very fond of the Pyrrhonism of Bayle and reached its full 'modern pagan' outlook in the new scepticism of Hume,[34] the Enlightenment as a whole did not renege the tradition of modern rationalism started in 'the century of genius' – the age of Galileo, Descartes and Newton. The *philosophes* put Newton's science well above Cartesian physics; but they had no qualms about upholding the *Discourse on Method*. The *Encyclopédie* noticed that Locke himself – the *philosophes*' master in psychology and epistemology – had been rescued from the barrenness of Oxford philosophy by his acquaintance with Descartes' revolution in cognitive strategy.

It seems, therefore, wise to take what we might call the Hazard problem with a pinch of salt; for whatever else it may have been, 'the crisis of European mind' in late baroque days was less than an epistemic mutation. Cognitive change there was, and structural change – but not to the point of bringing about a changeover. Yet, *why, in heaven's name, should we restrict the concept of epistemic breaks to epistemic earthquakes*? Why should we ignore the de-Cartesianization of physics, metaphysics and psychology as a peripheral affair, on the grounds that the classical age was a single episteme, embracing both Descartes and Condillac, Leibniz and the idéologues? Foucault shaped his epistemic landscapes with too dramatic contrasts; let's put some slopes where he sees only precipices, the all-or-nothing of mountains and plains. Miel is right to re-inspect what Hazard sensed without explaining: the metamorphosis of Western rationalism since around 1690. And the transformation of the Western thought at the threshold of the eighteenth century is a powerful argument against a monolithic view of epistemes.

Arguably, the 1690 mild break constitutes a qualified discontinuity within the early modern knowledge structure. Obviously, it's no good to dismiss this discontinuity – as indeed, in Foucault's view, so many continuities – as a sheer 'surface effect'. Rather, we'd better meditate on Bachelard – the Master of Break Theory – and acknowledge once and for all the occurrence of ruptures also *within* a given episteme. Actually, Bachelard went as far as accepting them even within the same thinker's work – a possibility that Althusser made famous with his thesis on the epistemological break between the young Marx and *Capital's* Marx.

Clearly, there is much with which Foucaldian archaeology cannot cope in the historical record of science and thought. Disturbing phenomena both between and within Foucault's epistemes simply don't fit in his own definition of historical knowledge paradigms. Let us now round up our appraisal by considering the philosophical outline of *Les Mots et les choses*. We have seen that Foucault is consistently uninterested in cognitive growth. He is not a bit concerned with the truth of knowledge. In the archaeology of epistemes, knowledge is 'envisioned apart from all criteria having reference to its rational value';[35] what the archaeologist, as distinct from the epistemologist, does is merely to ascertain some historical conditions of possibility of a number of knowledge forms, in total disregard of the latter's 'growing perfection' – in other words, of their increase in truth, rationally assessed. We may therefore say that Foucault's analysis does not care about the *story* of science – the tale of its progress in the path of testable, objective knowledge.

Now in the history of ideas, whoever shows little or no interest in the story of knowledge is generally thought to concentrate on the *history* of it. This is generally done by means of a *historist* approach, i.e., one intent on rendering and stressing the uniqueness of a certain epoch or cultural moment. In the history, as opposed to the story, of knowledge, conceptual structures are firmly set in their original context of meaning, regardless of their value for subsequent ages. However, here again, *The Order of Things* does not fit the bill. Besides deliberately ignoring the 'story' of science, the book often distorts the history of knowledge, as we saw in connection with its misinterpretations of Renaissance erudition or its underestimation of key aspects of early modern science. Neither a proper story nor an accurate history of knowledge, what is the real relevance, in global terms, of Foucault's 'archaeology'?

According to Hayden White, Foucault has launched a significant reorientation of historical inquiry. The conventional historian, argues White, is concerned to refamiliarize his readers with the past. Foucault, by contrast, strives to render the past unfamiliar.

Unwittingly, he rather follows Michelet's injunction to work for a 'resurrection' of past life, away from the placid, detached reconstructions sought by run-of-the-mill historiography. He is also close to Spengler's aim of revealing fundamental differences between historical cultures, instead of stressing their common traits. Like Burckhardt, the patron saint of Renaissance history, or Burckhardt's self-styled disciple, Huizinga, the great interpreter of the 'waning Middle Ages', Foucault's archaeology generates an 'alienating effect': it stages an intrinsically foreign and bizarre past.[36] At this juncture, some wits will feel tempted to add that, judging from his practice as a historian, Foucault surely makes the past unfamiliar – especially to professional historians, who often fail to recognize their subject matter in Foucault's garbled accounts of it. But let us not be mean. In defamiliarizing the past, Foucault is not being gratuitous. His point is, showing the strangeness of the worlds we have lost compels us moderns to take stock of our cultural identity through a realization of our distance from older forms of life and thought.

Alienating history, therefore, works as a main prop of the Foucaldian purpose: the critical grasp of modernity as a mode of existence. White puts Foucault in a structuralist wing which he labels 'dispersive' because it glories in the 'mystery' of the 'irreducible variety of human nature'. Instead of integrating differences into a common *humanitas*, 'dispersive' structuralists rejoice in cultural heterogeneity, in the social dispersal and differentiation of man.[37]

Doing history as defamiliarization from a 'dispersive' outlook has a serious implication: it *radically historicises* the objects under historiographic scrutiny. If you are looking into madness from a dispersive viewpoint, madness as such just vanishes: all that is left is one particular dated social game, a set of meanings labelled as such. That is why Foucault, who once wrote that in his *Histoire de la folie* he had sought to capture madness in itself, afterwards came to say that he did no such thing, but just drew an inventory of different epochal concepts of insanity. In 1961, he still talked of changing *perceptions* of madness. By 1970, he was arguing that such perceptions were no more than *inventions* of madness: the dispersive, *culturalist* outlook was now made fully explicit; realities were thoroughly dissolved into social concepts and social practices, historically given.

For the same reason, Paul Veyne, his fellow lecturer at the Collège de France (and the only outstanding historian who has poured unreserved praise on his work) hailed Foucault as a 'historian at his purest'. Foucault, claims Veyne, is the first true positivist, since the idea of historical objects independent of their (changing) social meanings is perfectly metaphysical – and Foucault taught us to get rid of it. This in turn he did because he took Nietzsche in earnest: things do not mean anything by themselves, but only insofar as they get a meaning from the historical creature, man. In a clever insight, Veyne regards Foucaldian archaeology as a scion of Nietzsche's *Genealogy of Morals* (II,12),[38] where Nietzsche asserts the essential 'fluidity' of all social meanings, equating the history of a 'thing' (sic) or of a custom with 'a continuous chain of ever new interpretations.'

In 'Nietzsche, Genealogy, History' – his main piece on Nietzsche – Foucault himself claimed that what distinguishes the 'genealogist' as critical historian is his awareness that things have no secret essence, no hidden origin, no noumenal ground.[39] History enjoys eternal youth (as Weber liked to say in his Nietzschean moments); it amounts to a permanent creation, knowing neither causal law nor final goal. Foucault's Nietzscheanism, though a belated avowal, helps in explaining his 'dispersive' outlook – his cold-shouldering of any structuralist search for invariant universals. Indeed, as early as 1967, he was marking off his enterprise from the structuralist paradigm: 'I differ from those who are called structuralist in that I am not greatly interested in the formal possibilities presented by a system such as language.'[40]

Nevertheless, one could never be too cautious about using Nietzsche to prop a theory of history as knowledge. For Nietzsche was not content to castigate, in the name of the vital interests of the present, 'philological', 'museological' historiography, history done with a desiccating, detached mood in an antiquarian spirit. He went on to slash the whole conception of historical objectivity itself, the idea – as he put it – of history as a 'mirror' of events (*Genealogy*, III, 26). Nietzsche attacked two kinds of 'specular' historiography:

'ascetic' academic narratives and 'aesthetic' evocations of the past; the method of Ranke and the art of Renan. But in both cases he disparaged mirror-like objectivity as nihilism – the ugliest sin in the Nietzschean code of life. Therefore, the upshot of Nietzsche's onslaught on the 'burden of history' was a wilful undermining of *every* historiographic concern for the truth of the past – a concern which, understandably, Veyne is not prepared to throw overboard. Nietzsche may free history from determinist metaphysics, but he also kills the quest for objectivity in the name of the higher rights of 'life'. Has he not taught that truth is not objectivity but a will to 'justice' (*Thoughts Out of Season*, II,6)? Justice, to be sure, in the hands of hanging judges, strong personalities whose very vitality puts them high above the mass of mankind. In such a climate of thought, truth is overpowered by wanton will – and history as a former knowledge becomes just a free-for-all for warring perspectives. To put it in a nutshell, Nietzsche the anti-determinist may serve the historian; but Nietzsche the perspectivist cuts the ground from under the historian's feet by destroying the rationale of his job: a reliable grasp of the past.

In this sense, unsurprisingly, Foucault sounds far more Nietzschean than Veyne. Consider his first, still untranslated discussion of the Master, 'Nietzsche, Freud, Marx' (1964), written as a communication to a symposium at Royaumont. It has been rightly said that in this paper Foucault attributes to the trio a position which in fact belongs eminently to Nietzsche. The position consists in holding every interpretandum *to be already an interpretation*. The death of interpretation, says Foucault, is the belief that there are signs of something, that is to say, some hidden essence waiting for us at the end of our interpretive journeys; 'the life of interpretation, on the contrary, is to believe that there are only interpretations'. Modern, critical knowledge is certainly an hermeneutic of depth; but that should not be construed as a search for deep structures; rather, we must realize the full analytic impact of what Nietzsche saw: that 'interpretation has [...] become an *infinite* task'.[41] This was read – in the prestigious and modish ambiance of the Royaumont symposia – in the teeth of the rising star of structuralism; and the text is almost contemporaneous with the writing of *Les Mots et les choses*.

The Nietzschean theme also helps us better to understand why Foucault can value the human sciences while at the same time denying them scientific status. He is not, of course, just saying that the human sciences don't achieve proper science as they are generally performed, i.e., with cloudy concepts and sloppy methods; what he denies is that they can *ever* be scientific. At the same time, however, he does *not* think of it as a handicap. The human sciences are no science, and man, at any rate, is a dwindling epistemic basis whence to conduct the business of knowledge; at most, some of them – the hypercritical 'counter-sciences', which make a living of watching the unconscious – are justified not because of what they assert but precisely because of their undoing the halfway interpretations of 'normal' social science. Yet far from despairing at such a cognitive plight, Foucault rejoices in it. Knowledge, for him, is not geared towards truth but to the everlasting *skepsis* of endless random interpretations – and his Nietzschean soul refuses to be depressed by it.

As Raymond Boudon and François Bourricaud notice in the entry on structuralism in their sharp *Dictionnaire critique de la sociologie*, Foucaldian history of science, by maintaining that the succession of epistemes is unintelligible, boils down, from a logical point of view, to a mere typology, with the additional disadvantage of ironing out many a complexity in the actual evolution of scientific thought. Still, Foucault seemed never to have really bothered about it: his Nietzschean posture allowed him a cynical flippancy as to the duties of scientific explanation. By definition, Nietzscheans do not get despondent just because they discover that knowledge is truthless, and truth itself just a pretence of the will-to-power.

Nevertheless, all in all, the ideological effect caused by *Les Mots et les choses*, albeit not as chilling as supposed by humanists disgruntled at the idea of man belittled, was not exactly exhilarating either. A modern *Phenomenology of the Spirit* in that it, too, traced an odyssey of thought through Western history, Foucault's book positively did not leave the reader exalting the present, nor indeed – as in Marx's erratum to Hegel – the future. Halfway between a bleak apocalypse and a truly joyful Dionysian surge, Foucault's conclusions seemed to point to further philosophical attitudes, as yet unassumed by him in the mid-sixties.

6. The ironic archive

Three years after *Les Mots et les choses*, Foucault published his own discourse on method: *The Archaeology of Knowledge* (1969). It is a curious work. Sometimes, it reads as a vindication of what he did in *Madness and Civilization*, *The Birth of the Clinic* and *The Order of Things*; sometimes, however, it seems to tap a new methodological (in fact, epistemological) awareness in order to criticize his own former shortcomings, though the object of his self-criticism seldom coincides with the numerous weaknesses pointed out by others in those historical studies. The most striking of these departures from earlier usage is the dropping of the concept of episteme, which *The Archaeology of Knowledge* replaces by a 'multiplicity of vertical systems'. But in fact Foucault is less interested in the break-up of epistemes than in asserting the primacy of discourse.

Here is, in effect, his new master concept, his pet idea in the interval between *The Order of Things* and his resuming his historical frescoes in the mid-seventies: *discourse*. Discourse, in *The Order of Things*, meant classical language, language reduced to the transparency of representation. But now Foucault warns that discourses are not to be taken as sets of signs referring to representations; rather, they are to be understood *as practices*. Naturally discourses employ signs, but what they do is *more* than use them to denote things.[1] Foucault's aim is precisely to describe this extra function of discourses. At the same time, however, he claims that this new perspective is 'what made it possible' for him to say what he did in his previous work.[2] Many a reader will find it hard to recognise discourses as practices among the epistemes of *Les Mots et les choses*, though it should not be that difficult to find something along this line in the social concepts on insanity underpinning rites of exclusion in *Madness and Civilization*.

At any rate, Foucault's project in *The Archaeology of Knowledge* is defined as 'a pure description of discursive events'.[3] The echo of phenomenological jargon (the 'pure description') should not mislead us: the archaeologist is being assigned to work far removed from the contemplation of things permanent. Discourses are highly precarious ensembles; they are made up of statements which live 'in a provisional grouping' as 'a population of events in the space of discourse'.[4] Throughout the book, the word *event* enjoys prominence. Foucault keeps up his old animus against continuous time of all sorts but he also seems intent on stressing the notion of irruptive, intersecting events despite every temptation to identify stable structures underneath a discursive surface.

Although discourses swarm with events, discursive 'regularities' and 'conditions of existence' can be elicited from them by the archaeologist. There are long, pedantic lucubrations on these quasi-structures in chapter 2 of *The Archaeology of Knowledge* ('the discursive regularities'). But Foucault is at pains to stress that the analysis he prescribes has nothing in common with the searches, inspired by structural linguistics, for One Big Urstruktur. There are several sentences sniping at the Saussurean tribe, e.g., 'one must suspend, not only the point of view of the signified [...] but also that of the signifier'.[5] Structuralists are treated as mere latter-day idealists. Nietzsche, by contrast, wins a widespread if largely tacit acceptance. In 1967, right between the publication of *Les Mots et les choses* and the completion of its methodological sequel, Foucault stated that archaeology owed more to Nietzschean genealogy than to structuralism.[6]

The Nietzschean twist explains, I think, the new anti-objectivist position of Foucault. In the *Archaeology* there is a pervasive polemic *against the object*, as a complement to the older structuralist criticism of the subject. Indeed, Foucault tries to show that the drawbacks in seeing discourse from the viewpoint of the subject are matched by too naive a stress on the opposite pole. He finds a paramount instance of unsatisfactory 'object' epistemology in Bachelard. The Bachelardian notion of 'epistemological obstacle', in particular, leading as it does to a 'psychoanalysis of objective knowledge', seems to witness the slip into the subject, who reappears through the backdoor: Bachelard resorts to the libido of the scientist in order to account for problems with the object of knowledge. Nor does the distancing from Bachelard stop at it. As Dominique Lecourt observed, Foucault also tends, in the *Archaeology*, to substitute the category of *irruption* for the Bachelardian concept of 'break', which is far too static to cope with the swarm of discursive events.[7]

Yet the real *bête noire* of the *Archaeology* is the history of ideas, which Foucault often caricatures. He explains that archaeology differs from the history of ideas in four aspects: (a) whereas the latter pursues themes and ideas expressed in documents the archaeologist seeks to examine the structure of documental discourse in itself; (b) the historian of ideas wants to trace the origin and fate of ideas, while the archaeologist fastens on a discourse for itself, regardless of what preceded and followed it; (c) the history of ideas looks for, and the archaeologist doesn't, psychological and sociological causes of intellectual events; (d) finally, the archaeologist of knowledge focuses on discourse as it is, without seeking, as the historian of ideas does, to grasp the ineffable moment of origin, the primitive intention of authors.[8]

In the first of these antitheses Foucault briefly opposes the treatment of discourse as *document* (history of ideas) to its analysis as a *monument* (archaeology of knowledge). Documents are conveyors of external reference; monuments are contemplated for themselves. It is the famous distinction made, in his *Meaning in the Visual Arts*, by the father of iconology, the art historian Erwin Panofsky (1892–1968).[9] Foucault does not mention him and may have drawn the same distinction independently. However, Panofsky was very much alive in Paris in the late sixties; a French translation of his *Studies in Iconology* (1939) had just been published by Gallimard (1967), receiving universal acclaim. But perhaps it's all for the best that Foucault doesn't quote him; for in Panofsky the document/monument difference has quite another meaning. Panofsky gives the example of a 1471 triptych in Rhineland and the contract commissioning it, with all the usual iconographic specifications ('in the centre piece, the Nativity; on the wings, St Peter and St Paul'). He says that the triptych, as an *object* of research for the art historian, is a monument, whereas the contract, being just an *instrument* of research (an aid for the interpretation of artistic intention and the knowledge of that time and place's aesthetic mores), works as a document. But Panofsky hastens to add that for the palaeographer or a historian of law, the triptych might very well become the document, and the contract the monument.

Moreover, he does not make his distinction in an either/or situation, so that either you deal with monuments and forget about documents or you busy yourself with documents, in which case you have no eye for monuments. On the contrary, iconology, as an art history method opposed to the *Formgeschichte* of Wölfflin,[10] strives to focus on the historical *content* of an artwork. Now Panofsky, following Charles Sanders Peirce, the American nineteenth-century philosopher who is considered the founder of non-Saussurean semiotics, defines the content, as distinct from the subject, of a work as that kind of meaning which the artwork *betrays* without *displaying*. Content is that meaning which 'shows through' a work of art without being shown in any ostensive way. Elements of content in this sense are national attitudes, class mentality, ideological backgrounds, etc. – in sum, everything that can condition in a more than trivial way the personality of the artist and through it get into the various strata of meaning of his work.[11] The aim of iconology is, therefore, emphatically historical and contextualist.[12] As such, iconology is a discipline which takes a path *opposite* to the anti-contextualist stance upheld by Foucault in contradistinction to the normal procedures of the history of ideas. It was not for nothing that Lévi-Strauss used Panofsky to chastise the formalist shortcomings of structuralist criticism.

Whether he liked it or not, in rejecting the contextual approach Foucault coincided with mainstream structuralism. He, too, was pitting 'immanent analysis' against a broader framework of interpretation, capable of integrating the focus on the monument with the awareness of its social and cultural environment. What disguises this kinship with formalism in Foucault's theory of discourse is, of course, its accent on discourse *as practice* – a conceptual overtone clearly beckoning to a non-formalist (Marxist) tradition. Furthermore, by using structuralism and the linguistic model as foils to his own methodological programme, Foucault gives the impression that archaeology and the structuralism, say, of literary criticism have little in common. In fact, however, they share a major perspective: the severance of 'immanent analysis' from a synthetic approach, resting on a wise balance between text and context as sources of meaning.

Curiously enough, such a balance was being urged, at precisely the time of Foucault's writing, by what may be called the Cambridge overhaul of methodology in the history of ideas – a critical task brilliantly performed, in the late sixties, by scholars such as John Dunn and especially Quentin Skinner.[13] Skinner has subjected the 'anachronistic mythologies' which infest the practice of the historiography of thought to a thorough and cogent scrutiny. To a certain extent, some of Foucault's more empirical-minded strictures tend to converge with Skinner's (e.g., his objections to the indiscriminate use of the notion of 'influence'). In general, however, Skinner's critique is conducted in terms which set it miles away from structuralist anti-subject hysteria and the *a priori* dismissal of authorial intentions. It points out the weaknesses of run-of-the-mill history of ideas without in the least jettisoning the legitimacy of its principle. The arbitrariness of Foucault's wholesale onslaught contrasts vividly with Skinner's careful analytical approach, adopted with a view to avoiding both the shortcomings of myopic textualism and the fallacies of reductionist contextualism. Surprisingly, the Cambridge papers on this important problematic get no mention either from Foucault or from Foucaldians.

Foucault claims that histories of ideas focus on authorship and novelty but end up in contradiction, for in seeking the roots of ideas (one of the consequences of their fascination with historical continuity) they paradoxically seize on what prevents ideas from being truly new. Against this focus on authors, novelty and continuity, archaeology stresses impersonality, regularities and discontinuities in discourse. Its main weapon is the concept of statement or enunciation (*énoncé*). Discursive formations are made of statements. Foucault defines the statement chiefly in a negative way, by telling us what it *isn't*. Statements as nuclei of discourse are neither logical propositions nor grammatical sentences or speech acts. Foucault illustrates the point by saying that a taxonomic table in a botanical textbook, or a genealogical tree, or an equation, consist of statements, but obviously not of sentences.[14] He is far less precise as to what statements *are*. He seems to think of them as 'functions' rather than 'things'; and they also are like 'events': material, but incorporeal. One arcane reason for their being unlike propositions is that they are, and the latter are not, under the sway of 'scarcity'. Would this be a nod towards Sartre's *Critique of Dialectical Reason*, where the scarcity category plays a pivotal role? Nevertheless, one thing seems clear: statements somehow evince what is involved in the production of signs. Insofar as they are composed of statements, 'discursive practices' are sets 'of anonymous and historical rules, always specific as to time and place, and which, for a given period and within a social, economic, geographic or linguistic zone, define the framework within which the enunciative functions are exercised'.[15] It sounds more like a tautology than like a definition, but the general idea is there: 'historical rules' governing discourse. The same notion reappears when Foucault uses what is, together with discourse, 'statement' and 'event', the fourth big word of his *Archaeology of Knowledge*: *archive*. For the 'archive' is 'the first law of what can be said', 'the system that governs the appearance of statements as unique events'.[16] The archive is neither the linguistic system nor the tradition, the heavy corpus of discourses in a given civilization.[17] Rather, it corresponds to the 'play of rules which determines within a culture the appearance and disappearance of statements'.[18]

The 'archive', then (if we really can pierce through the fog of Foucault's indefinitions), is a machine generating social – as opposed to linguistic – meaning. It is, in any case, an 'historical *a priori*'. The archaeologist, needless to say, is an archivist. It also goes without saying that in his task – the analysis of discourses made up of event-statements – he blithely surrenders to that allergy to the subject which is the trade-mark of structuralisms. An archivist, after all, does not busy himself with personalities, just with documents and their classifications. So the archaeologist as archivist does not stoop to find out who said or wrote what to whom: this would imply subjects, hence, anthropologism, a humanist delusion and an idealist vice. A text of 1969, 'What is an Author?', makes clear that we must get rid of our habit of looking for an author's authority, and show instead how the power of discourse constrains both author and his utterances.[19] Once or twice, the dismissal of the subject sounds like common-sense but trivial logic, as when Foucault claims that, whereas the foreword to a book of mathematics explaining the author's intentions plainly has a subject in its author, the theorems therein don't, insofar as they refer to their own logical order.[20] More often than not, however, the subject-bashing is decreed by speculative diktats such as '... the subject is necessarily situated and dependent'.[21] Why 'necessarily' dependent? We are not enlightened. As for structuralists, they need no enlightenment in this regard: they just 'know' that it is so. Delendum subjectum!

Finally, the theory of discourse-archive refuses to choose between science and ideology. The section 'Science and Knowledge' (IV,6) warns that the role of ideology in science (a large one, says Foucault, in medicine or political economy) does not in the least diminish to the extent that scientific rigour and falsifiability grow. The whole drift of these pages suggests that the only way to fight the ideological action of a given science is not to unmask its philosophical assumptions or cultural biases, even less to pin down its errors and contradictions, but rather to question its system of object-constitution and its 'theoretical choices', that is to say, to question science *as a practice* amidst other practices. Once again, like in *The Order of Things*, Foucault shows no interest in the 'rational value' of science, yet frankly admits – indeed, seems to encourage – an *a priori* questioning of scientific views.

An archaeology of knowledge could do better than to distrust knowledge in such an *a priori* way. No wonder Foucault's archaeology, as 'a discourse about discourses',[22] ends up by confessing that, 'for the moment', it, 'far from specifying the locus from which it speaks, avoids the ground on which it could lean'. Such are the central words in the conclusion of the book, which takes the form of a dialogue. Archaeology cannot produce its own title of legitimacy as a critical theory. Must we laud its modesty or regret that, in the name of a groundless stance, so many established ways to knowledge (as poor history of ideas) were wholly rejected, with so little sound or solid offered in their stead?

Much of the *Archaeology* (despite its plodding arid prose) is written with the pen of irony. Sometimes even a rare glimmer of witty flippancy shines, as when towards the close of the introduction Foucault replies to an imaginary critic nagging him on his changes of perspective: 'Do not ask me who I am and [...] to remain the same: leave it to our bureaucrats and our police to see that our papers are in order.' Professors at the Collège de France or other academic Olympuses regarding themselves as maverick bohemians at war with bureaucracy and *les flics* are a permanent possibility among French intellectualdom, a bourgeois stratum dying to pass for an intelligentsia. But generally speaking, the irony of the book is made of sterner stuff. It lies, as Allan Megill very aptly said, 'in the fact that whereas it appears to be a rigorously objective attempt to articulate a new scientific methodology, it is actually an attempt to demolish everything that has hitherto gone under the name of science.'[23] And so it is.

We are delighted to learn that the archivist, for all his dullness, is an ironist. We suspect he became one because, as he crossed the distance from *Les Mots et les choses* to his own discourse on method, he plunged deeper and deeper in the radical perspectivism of Nietzsche while at the same time keeping his old concern with the rather un-Nietzschean subject of science and its history. Thus the archive, the machine of discursive meaning, is at bottom a *Weltspiel*, a worldplay, a ludic cosmos ever engendering new active interpretations (discourses as practices) of life and society. And it is indeed a highly ironic archive: with it, no meaning remains stable, no truth is better than the next one. In no time the leader of the growing legion of neo-Nietzscheans, Gilles Deleuze, would salute in Foucault the conquistador of 'this *terra incognita* where a literary form, a scientific proposition, a daily sentence, a schizophrenic nonsense, etc. are equally statements, despite their lack of a common measure'.[24] As Deleuze explains in the same breath, the flaw in Bachelard is that he still insisted on separating science from poetry. Nobody runs such a risk with neo-Nietzscheans.

Foucault's inaugural lecture at the Collège de France, *L'Ordre du discours* (1971; the title was mistranslated into *The Discourse on Language*) provided the perfect transition from an archaeological to a genealogical problematics by explicitly linking the concept of discourse with power and control. 'In every society', says Foucault, 'the production of discourse is at once controlled, selected, organized and redistributed according to a certain number of procedures.'[25] Such procedures comprehend external controls, internal rules and the regulation of access to knowledge.

External controls work as kinds of *exclusion*: *prohibition* of expression (in our age chiefly on expressions of desire and power); *rejection*, as in the isolation of the language of madness; or the opposition between true and false, maintained by the *will to truth* of modern man – a mere mask, of course, of his will to power. Modern man, incidentally, is slackening off prohibitions and rejections but holds fast to his will to truth. Internal rules are procedures of discourse-making that foist continuity on discourse. Thus the practice of commentary strives to rivet discourse on original meaning; rules relative to authorship impose the myth of the unity of consciousness; and rules classifying discourses maintain borders between disciplines, stifling vital questions in the process (e.g., Mendel's discoveries were long the victims of compartmentalized biological work). Finally, access to discourse as knowledge is also an object of control, most conspicuously in the closed-shop customs of professional discourse (e.g., doctors) and more generally in the educational system itself, 'a political means of maintaining or modifying the appropriation of discourse'. Nothing in all this is actually contradicted by the elastic obscure concepts of *The Archaeology of Knowledge*. Did not the latter harbour the injunction to 'conceive discourse as a violence that we do to things'?[26] Yet one can see that this list of rules of exclusion, reading as it does as a catalogue of *gauchiste* grievances in the spirit of 1968, is a long way from the elusiveness of 'discourse as practice'. Now the name of the game is power.

7. Charting carceral society

After his methodological pause in *The Archaeology of Knowledge* and *L'Ordre du discours*, Foucault resolutely turned to a 'political' history of knowledge. The latter work definitely cast suspicion upon the very concept of truth, which was merely 'suspended' in the *Archaeology*. Hereafter, epistemological categories tended to be frankly 'politicized'. It was no wonder that, at the same time, Foucault redefined the role of intellectuals in the perspective of veritable eclipse of theory. Discussing intellectuals and power with Deleuze in 1972, Foucault declared that the masses don't need intellectuals to know. Therefore, the role of the intellectual is no longer to provide theory for the enlightenment of the masses; and the role of theory, in turn, changes: it is no longer a striving to attain consciousness but simply a struggle 'for undermining and capturing authority'. Theory is not like a pair of glasses; it is rather like a pair of guns; it does not enable one to see better but to fight better. Intellectuals ought to be struggling against the forms of power they are involved with: knowledge, truth, discourse.[1]

Note that this is miles away from the 'Left Marxist' *conflation* of theory into praxis, best exemplified by Gramsci or the young Lukács: here we have no welding of theory and practice, but rather a *collapse* of theory into practice. Praxis ceases to have a theoretical ballast: each social practice runs its own show, and 'theoretical practice' – the intellectuals' job – would just be one of them, were it not for the fact that, in a sense, it is bound to be an unhappy practice, doomed to self-suspicion and bad consciousness. For Foucault's merciless debunking of the intellectual function ends up in more than one masochistic note. Fortunately, it is now a long time since the French establishment learned that the best way to deal with its intellectuals' tantrums (or autophagic fits) is to behave in a manner reminiscent of that old Paris joke: the masochist said to the sadist, 'Hit me!' But the sadist retorted, 'No!'

The first instalment in Foucault's political history of truth of knowledge came without stint: three hundred-odd pages on 'the birth of prison', under the title *Discipline and Punish*, a good though not literal translation of *Surveiller et punir*, 1975 (the German edition, however, rendered both verbs: *Uberwachen und Strafen*). Foucault once called it 'my first book' and not without reason: for it is a serious contender for first place among his books as far as language and structure, style of presentation and ordering of parts go. It is not a bit less engrossing than *Madness and Civilization*, nor less original than *The Order of Things*. Once more Foucault unearths the most unexpected primary sources; once again his reinterpretation of the historical record is as bold as thought-provoking. If in periodization the essay on the birth of the prison recalls *The Birth of the Clinic*, covering roughly the same time-span, from mid-eighteenth to mid-nineteenth century, in breadth of scope it is almost the equal of *Les Mots et les choses*. Knowledge on life, labour and language gave a broad range to the subject matter of the earlier book: now the idea of a basic isomorphic role played by prison, factory, hospital and school lends *Discipline and Punish* a similar catholicity of concern, though this time the author, no doubt wisely, chose to keep analysis firmly centred to just one of these institutional areas: the penal establishments and discourses.

Any reader of Foucault is likely to recall the graphic image of the lazar-houses turned into bedlams at the outset of *Madness and Civilization*. *Discipline and Punish* gets a still more sensational prelude: the spectacular execution of the would-be regicide Damiens, who in the year of Our Lord 1757 failed to take the life of, or indeed to hurt, Louis XV. Foucault dwells on the ghastly particulars of the racking of Damiens, who had his flesh torn from breast and limbs with red-hot pincers, the hand with which he attempted *lèse-majesté* burnt with sulphur, and then his body, or what was left of it, quartered by four horses and eventually consumed by fire – all this being done before the good people of Paris, who wouldn't miss such fun for all the tea in China.

Three reigns plus one long revolution and the Empire later, in the truly bourgeois days of Louis Philippe, Fieschi, another would-be regicide, was executed without all that grisly pomp and circumstance. At the same time – as shown in a fastidious set of rules drawn up for a contemporary House of Young Prisoners in Paris – an amount of inventiveness by no means inferior to the plethora of ritual cruelty displayed in the maiming of Damiens was employed in the meticulous schedule of the prisoners' day. Lavish torture in the past gave way to punctilious over-regulation by the 1830s. Foucault's aim is to describe these different 'penal styles', these contrasting punitive regimes. The key change was signalled by the disappearance of physical torture. Post-Napoleonic France knew nothing even remotely similar to the public racking of Damiens; yet she kept over forty thousand Frenchmen and Frenchwomen in gaol (approximately one prisoner per 600 inhabitants). Punishment as a gruesome spectacle receded; large prisons as a conspicuous element in the urban landscape spread their towers all over the bourgeois West. 'Carceral society' was born.

The first penal age portrayed by Foucault is the era of public torture. Its setting is the scaffold, the sovereign its central power-figure. The law being the king's will, breaking the law was to attack the monarch personally. Hence the right of the sovereign to pay back in kind, in savage retribution. To be sure, in everyday penal practice Dantesque torture and public execution were far from frequent. At the court of the Châtelet, seat of the Paris provostry, less than 10 per cent of the sentences passed between 1755 and 1785 amounted to capital punishment. Actually most sentences imposed banishment or fines. However, a great many of the non-corporal sentences, e.g., all sentences to the galleys, were accompanied by smaller penalities with some degree of torture, like pillory, carcan, flogging or branding; thus every serious punishment ultimately involved an element of 'supplice', i.e., of torture.

Torture was also employed, of course, as a means of eliciting confessions, so that a ritual truth – an admission of guilt literally extracted from the accused – could crown and justify a display of force often quite disproportionate to the crime committed. Yet this awe-inspiring violence, this lurid epic of grim punishment, was also in fact rather limited. As a punitive regime, it was as intermittent as spectacular. Its very object – the criminal subject's body – imposed narrow bounds on royal reprisals. And victims had the right to curse the power that broke them: 'The public execution allowed the luxury of these momentary saturnalia, when nothing remained to prohibit or to punish. Under the protection of imminent death, the criminal could say everything and the crowd cheered. [...] In these executions, which ought to show only the terrorizing power of the prince, there was a whole aspect of the carnival, in which rules were inverted, authority mocked and criminals transformed into heroes.'[2]

Always fond – as a good structuralist – of 'symmetrical inversions', Foucault states that 'the body of the condemned' (the title of his first chapter) is the opposite pole of the 'King's body'. He is referring to the medieval legal and political concept analysed by Ernst Kantorowicz (1895–1963) in his classic *The King's Two Bodies* (1957; not, as Foucault's note says, 1959). According to the myth of the twin-born king, it was assumed that sovereigns had two bodies. One was the natural body, subject to decay. The other was the *aevum*: a holy, mystical, eternal body, a secular perpetuity through which the dignity of kingship survived all human frailty and monarchic misfortune. Kantorowicz showed how deeply this mythical idea penetrated into English legal thought. It was actually still alive in the royalist literature of Cromwellian England. Some copies of the *Eikon Basilike* include a long poem, 'Majesty in Misery', ascribed to the unfortunate Charles I. In it the deposed sovereign, judged and condemned 'in the name of the king' precisely by means of the two-bodies theory, makes a bitter, poignant comment on his fate in terms couched in that self-same ideology:

> With my own power my majesty they wound,
> In the King's name the king himself uncrowned.
> So does the dust destroy the diamond.[3]

Foucault's point is that just as the royal *aevum* gave the sovereign a sacral body, symbol of the body politic, so the scaffold had in its victim a body which was the very antithesis of the right and might of royal power.

Thereupon came the Enlightenment and its rational reformism. A number of lawyers and magistrates as well as the growing 'public opinion' in the age of Voltaire and Beccaria realized that the violent but irregular system of punishment as exemplary and excessive retribution was not just inhuman: it was also failing as a deterrent of crime. In addition, one could never be too sure about the direction taken by the mob's feelings excited by public executions. Criminal justice, it came to be thought, should be made to seek punishment, not revenge. With the vogue of social contract theories, crime came to be regarded not as an attack on the sovereign but as a breach of the social covenant, thereby jeopardizing society as a whole. New methods of punishment were proposed, which would at once redress the wrong done to the community and restore the offender to his proper place within it. Therefore the prime concern of penal authority became the mind, not the body, of the criminal. While torture was to be abolished, 'a whole technology of representatives' – remember the representational character of the classical episteme – was devised; its purpose was to bring home to prisoners the logic of their punishment. Much care was given to establishing a rational correspondence between kinds of offence and grades of punishment; sentences should at all costs avoid being arbitrary. The eighteenth-century reformers fully shared the taxonomic bent of their age: they sought to draw a table where each crime and its penalty would be perfectly legible. They conceived of a detailed classification of crimes and criminals, within a horizon of individualized treatment of each law-breaker. And the overarching aim of their humanitarianism was a consideration of social utility. Punishment should not breed terror but penance. Sanctions should be as didactic as well-founded and impartial, or else the point of social reintegration would be lost. Thus several strands of classical thought – social contract theory, utilitarianism, the semiotics of representation – were combined in a new rationale for punishment. By developing theories of mental representations connected with a doctrine of enlightened self-interest, late eighteenth century thinkers such as the *idéologues* provided the West, on the eve of the spread of industrialism, with a 'a sort of general recipe for the exercise of power over men: the "mind" as a surface of inscription for power [...]; the submission of bodies through the control of ideas'.[4]

Foucault is clear: at bottom, humanitarianism, in the Enlightenment, counts less than will to power. Underneath its noble ideals of human emancipation, the Enlightenment defined new 'moral technologies' conducive to a degree of social control far greater than was the case in traditional societies. The penal reformers did not as much want to punish less as 'to punish better; to punish with an attenuated severity perhaps, but in order to punish with more universality and necessity; to insert the power to punish more deeply in the social body.'[5]

The standard image of the Enlightenment usually stresses its Utopian components. Foucault would agree. The only difference is that he has a different view of the Enlightenment's Utopia. To him, it was a totalitarian blueprint:

> Historians of ideas usually attribute the dream of a perfect society to the philosophers and jurists of the eighteenth century; but there was also a military dream of society; its fundamental reference was not to the state of nature, but to the meticulously subordinated cogs of a machine, not to the primal social contract, but to permanent coercions, not to fundamental rights, but to indefinitely progressive forms of training, not to general will but to automatic docility.[6]

From the machine-like empire based on national discipline dreamt of by the tactician Guibert to Napoleon's love for organizational detail, a whole array of disciplinary mirages is considered to have adumbrated bourgeois order in the nineteenth-century Western society. Modern man, writes Foucault, was born in a welter of regulations: meticulous rules and subrules, fussy inspections, 'the supervision of the smallest fragment of life and of the body [...] in the context of the school, the barracks, the hospital or the workshop'.[7] This grey Utopia of the Enlightenment did not of course come wholly true. Yet Foucault thinks that it did manage to pervade large areas of modern culture, and that the prison was the field par excellence of its application. *Discipline and Punish* suggests strong connections between disciplinary ideas from the classical age and the rise of a 'surveillance' model of penal institution – the birth of the prison in the modern sense – throughout the early and mid-nineteenth century.

Like the systems devised by the enlightened reformers, the penitentiary aimed at the moral transformation of the criminal. It also had some real precedents, based on paid work, moral exhortation and a whole set of duties and prohibitions, in Dutch and Flemish correctional workhouses (from the Amsterdam Rasphuis, opened in 1596, to the Maison Force at Ghent) and in English eighteenth-century prison reform. When the loss of the American colonies put an end to deportation, Blackstone, the foremost jurist of his time in England, opted for 'reforming' incarceration. Then, in Quaker Philadelphia, at Walnut Street prison, (1790), the modern penitentiary was launched: cells, moral guidance, work as both a means to rehabilitation and a source of economic support for the prison itself, and last but not least – full dossiers and thorough observation of each inmate. On top of which came the acknowledged autonomy of penal authorities, to whom society delegated a professional 'right to punish' for the sake of the common good. Prisons became the seat of regimes of total, uninterrupted surveillance. Bentham's 'panopticon' – an annular architectural contraption with a watchful tower in its middle – was quickly adopted. With the panopticon or its equivalents, each cell stands within the reach of a central, invisible inspection. Prisoners, not knowing when they are observed, have to behave at all times as though they were being watched. The compact building of old prisons, 'burying' criminals together in depths of stone and darkness (I cannot help thinking of them ascending towards light in the second act of Beethoven's *Fidelio*), was replaced by lighter edifices where inmates were isolated – and permanently inspected. Exit the hidden dungeon, enter the transparent cell.

But Foucault doesn't stop here. He sets out to persuade us that Bentham's panopticon, no matter how seldom or how imperfectly realized, is but an epitome of a widespread trend in bourgeois society – the *disciplinary* drive. The panopticon, in sum, was just a graphic instance of '*panopticism*' (a label actually used by Foucault as the title of a long, crowning chapter in *Discipline and Punish*). Just as the 'political dream' of traditional society, as expressed in the exile of lepers, was the vision of a pure community, the political dream of modern, bourgeois culture is 'a disciplined society'. And its moulding power embraces several key institutions:

> [...] project the subtle segmentations of discipline on to the confused space of internment, combine it with the methods of analytical distribution proper to power, individualize the excluded, but use procedures of individualization to mark exclusion – this is what was operated regularly by disciplinary power from the beginning of the nineteenth century in the psychiatric asylum, the penitentiary, the reformatory, the approved school and, to some extent, the hospital. Generally speaking, all the authorities exercising individual control function according to a double mode; that of binary division and branding (mad/sane; dangerous/harmless; normal/abnormal); and that of coercive assignment, of differential distribution (who he is; where he must be; how he is to be characterized; how he is to be recognized; how a constant surveillance is to be exercised over him in an individual way, etc.).[8]

For discipline to obtain, four main conditions had to be provided. The first was *an art of spatial distribution*, most visible in techniques of functional segregation, as shown in the cellular space, first developed by military hospitals such as the naval one at Rochefort. The Ecole Militaire in Paris was also built on a monastic model. In both cases, cells and surveillance were closely linked. The *Encyclopédie* article on 'manufacture' recommended skilled surveillance as an indispensable method in industrial production. Foucault describes the Oberkampf factory at Jouy (c. 1790) as a telling case of *avant-la-lettre* Taylorism: the 'manufactory' was split up into a series of workshops, each with a different function (printers, engravers, dyers, etc.) and all placed under prompt and careful supervision. But cells or no cells, the ideal of disciplinary space made its way. Barracks and boarding schools were regarded as much better means to deal with soldiers and youngsters.

The second prop to discipline was the *control of activity* proper: scheduling the daily activities of workers or inmates, imposing regularity on behaviour down to the very movements of the body. Foucault dwells on classical prescriptions as to the position to be maintained in handwriting, the precise gestures to be made in carrying and loading weapons, or the articulation of bodily movements in view of machine rhythms in the factory. The third prop was *exercise*. Long a religious practice, cherished in Rhenish mysticism or Jesuit asceticism (cf. Loyola's 'spiritual exercises'), it ceased to be just a means of ordering earthly time with a view to reach salvation to become a powerful tool in 'the political technology of the body and of duration', mainly in armies and schools.

Finally, the fourth instrument of discipline was the 'combination of forces' or *tactics*. Individuals were to be placed or moved together with great skill and precision. Individual bravery, for example, became less of a concern, to the military mind, than the role of an individual body, orderly combined with others in action. Similar procedures, of course, were ingrained in factories and schools.

All in all, the cell and the form, the time-table and the gesture-codes, drill and tactics converged to create 'docile bodies' – the stuff of disciplinary society.[9] Foucault makes an important historical point: whereas at first disciplines were expected to neutralize dangers, as the Ancien Régime gave way to modern bourgeois society, they came to play a more *positive* role. At one time military discipline was envisaged just as a means to prevent looting or desertion; then it became a method to increase armed capability. The same goes for schools and workplaces. Watchful organization of work was intended to avoid theft or loss of raw material; in time, it was directed at the enhancement of skills, speeds and productivity. Thus the same disciplines acquired quite new functions.

Discipline based on surveillance needed to delegate supervision. Hierarchic observation became a rule, both at the factory (as required by the complication of the division of labour) and at the school (where pupils were chosen to act as heads of form), let alone in the forces. Foucault spends some pages describing the grading of surveillance power. Moreover, the disciplinary society did not operate only in terms of formal control and regulations; it also employed a 'micro-penality' geared to a thorough scanning of conduct:

> [...] the workshop, the school, the army were subject to a whole micro-penality of time (latenesses, absences, interruptions of tasks), activity (inattention, negligence, lack of zeal), of behaviour (impoliteness, disobedience), of speech (idle chatter, insolence), of the body ('incorrect' attitudes, irregular gestures, lack of cleanliness), of sexuality (impurity, indecency). At the same time, by way of punishment, a whole series of subtle procedures was used, from light physical punishment to minor deprivations and petty humiliations. It was a question both of making the slightest departures from correct behaviour subject to punishment, and of giving a punitive function to apparently indifferent elements of the disciplinary apparatus: so that, if necessary, everything might serve to punish the slightest thing; each subject finds himself caught in a punishable, punishing universality.[10]

The web of discipline aims at generalizing the *homo docilis* required by 'rational', efficient, 'technical' society: an obedient, hard-working, conscience-ridden, useful creature, pliable to all modern tactics of production and warfare. And ultimately the main way to achieve docility is the moral pressure of continuous comparison between good and bad citizens, young or adult: discipline thrives on '*normalizing judgement*'. Bourgeois society bred an obsession with the norm, from the 'écoles normales' to the keeping up of standards in industrial production and the concern with general norms of health in the modern hospital.

Normalizing judgement and hierarchical surveillance are particularly conspicuous in *examinations*.[11] Exams lie at the heart of discipline, as one of its most ritualized procedures, precisely because in them the need to observe and supervise and the right to punish are deeply entwined with one another. Nowhere does the superimposition of power and knowledge assume such a perfect visibility.

But examination goes beyond exams. Foucault notices that it became a practice for doctors in the modern, rather than the traditional, hospital. Still more generally, he points out the use of files and reports throughout so many areas of social activity. He then stresses the changed function in the transcription of human lives: the contrast, that is, between the chronicle, with its accent on the heroic and memorable, and the file, measuring up observance as deviation from the norm. Contending that disciplinary methods 'lowered the threshold of describable individuality' by substituting the calculable man for the memorable ancestor, he twice suggests that social science rose in league with the objectifying gaze of disciplinary, normalizing, examination. The cradle of the sciences of man, he surmises, is perhaps to be found in 'the "ignoble" archives' of clinical and penal observation; panoptic methods in the disciplinary society have made a science of man possible; 'knowable man (soul, individuality, consciousness, conduct, whatever it is called) is the object-effect of this analytical investment, of this domination-observation.'[12]

Foucault's endeavour, in his final chapter on the birth of modern prison (i.e., prison in the first half of the nineteenth century), is to look at the penitentiary from the vantage point of this socio-epistemology of discipline. Foucault invites us to pause and think of the monotonous criticisms addressed at the prison's failure to deter criminality and correct criminals. Should we not, asks he, reverse the problem? Questions which remain unanswered for so long generally tend to be the wrong kind of question. So perhaps the prison did not fail, after all: only, it succeeded where one did not search for its success. Prisons did not so much fail to eliminate crime as *succeeded in producing delinquency*, and not just in the empirical sense of fostering so many *societates sceleris* when rehabilitation was expected, but precisely in the perspective of power/knowledge: prisons encapsulate punitive systems which, in Foucault's claim, are less intended to eliminate offences than 'to distinguish them, to distribute them, to use them', and in so doing 'tend to assimilate the transgression of the laws in a general tactics of subjection'.[13]

For Foucault makes no bones about it: we live – as direct heirs to the impulses and institutions first manifested in the high tide of rising of bourgeois society – under a 'universal reign of the normative' dominated by agents of normalcy and surveillance: the teacher-judge, the doctor-judge, the educator-judge, the social-worker-judge. And such a social world is plainly 'a carceral network' in 'compact or disseminated forms'. Whilst in the days of yore the criminal, as the sinner, was an outcast, in the realm of discipline the delinquent is not exactly outside the law: 'he is, from the very outset, in the law, at the very heart of the law, or at least in the midst of those mechanisms that transfer the individual imperceptibly from discipline to the law, from deviation to offence.' The 'carceral system', therefore, extends '*well beyond legal imprisonment*'; prison is at bottom just its 'pure form' within a continuum of disciplinary apparatuses and 'regional' institutions. In its function, then, 'the power to punish is not essentially different from that of curing or educating'; and by the same logic, 'by means of a carceral continuum, the authority that sentences infiltrates all those other authorities that supervise, transform, correct, improve'. Thanks to 'the carceral texture of society', there is a ceaseless 'mingling' of 'the art of rectifying and the right to punish'.[14] And so on and so forth, ad nauseam. The rhetorical peak is the often quoted: 'Is it surprising that prisons resemble factories, schools, barracks, hospitals, which all resemble prisons?'[15] – the very closing sentence of the 'panopticism' chapter.

Discipline and Punish, as a work of (philosophical) history, is at once less reckless and more shoddy than *The Order of Things*. The fourth and final part, on the birth of the modern prison proper, has been widely considered a sloppy anti-climax to the rhetoric of 'panopticism'. Yet in general Foucault is now much more careful; for instance, he does not put such a rash emphasis on absolute breaks, and in fact has a lot to say about transitions and continuities from one age into another, as we saw in his description of precedents of the disciplinary apparatuses ('dispositifs'). One has only to read his pithy aside on the role of Napoleon in historical mythology – a figure combining the ritual exercise of sovereignty of traditional monarchy with the strenuousness of daily surveillance[16] – to realize how fine a grasper of transitions Michel Foucault, the master of caesurae, can be. Nor does he forget, this time, prudently to limit his geography to

France, thus avoiding one of the most glaring pitfalls of both *Madness and Civilization* and *The Order of Things*: the lack of geographical differentiation in their main historical concepts.[17] Sometimes he keeps close to empirical history in a truly insightful way, as witnessed by his brief remarks on the debate on carceral reform under Louis Philippe. Then, while Charles Lucas (often quoted by Foucault) inspired a monastic model of 'maison centrale', based on work in common and absolute silence, Tocqueville and others favoured the Pennsylvanian regime of utter isolation. The wave of prison revolts following the adoption of *maisons centrales* and the general agitation in France in the early 1840s led to the victory of the segregationists, until a penitentiary congress in 1847 ruled out their option.[18] Passages like this humble footnote grant us a glimpse of 'another' *Birth of the Prison*: less theatrical and rhetorical, but not a bit less fascinating.

Alas, this was not to be. Foucault definitely prefers ideological drama to the wayward contingencies of actual history. His indictment of the rise of the bourgeoisie is typical:

> Historically, the process by which the bourgeoisie became in the course of the eighteenth century the politically dominant class was masked by the establishment of an explicit, coded and formally egalitarian juridical framework, made possible by the organization of a parliamentary, representative régime. But the development and generalization of disciplinary mechanisms constituted the other, dark side of these processes. The general juridical form that guaranteed a system of rights that were egalitarian in principle was supported by these tiny, everyday, physical mechanisms, by all those systems of micro-power that are essentially non-egalitarian and asymmetrical that we call the disciplines.[19]

And Foucault adds that while the social contract may have been regarded as the 'ideal' (the French original says it better: the 'imagined') source of power, panopticism was the real thing – a widespread, universal technique of coercion.

The bourgeoisie imposed a double standard in the penal field. On the one hand, it promoted penal reform in its own interest. Codification, fair trials, rational criteria for the weighing of evidence, presumption of innocence and a reasonable correspondence between crime and penalty all worked in favour of an educated upper class, jealous of its rights and possessing wealth, prestige and political clout. On the other hand, the same ruling class invented surveillance, imprisonment and countless repressive devices as a way of containing social unrest and a means of training a work force.

There is, of course, more than a grain of truth in both scenarios. But Foucault's view of the whole process is simply too Manichaean. Why should the historian choose between the angelic image of a demo-liberal bourgeois order, unstained by class domination, and the hellish picture of ubiquitous coercion? Is not the actual historical record a mixed one, showing real libertarian and equalizing trends beside several configurations of class power and coercive cultural traits?

However, bourgeoisie-bashing is not, as we saw, the central message of the book. The worst blows are addressed not as much at the bourgeois as at the Enlightenment, both as an age and as a long-run phenomenon, a cultural evolution still with us: the Enlightenment, alias modernity. Commenting on a contemporary discussing Bentham's panopticon, Foucault embarks on an antithesis between ancient society, 'a civilization of spectacle', and our society, which is 'one not of spectacle, but of surveillance'. In a world without community and public life at its centre, but, on the one hand, private individuals and, on the other, the state, relations are regulated in a form that is the exact reverse of the spectacle. We are much less Greek than we like to believe, says Foucault. Behind our 'great abstraction of exchange' we forcibly train bodies as manipulable useful forces. Our broad circuits of communication serve the centralization (sic) of knowledge; and with us 'the play of signs defines the anchorages of power'.

Ultimately, Foucault sees the punitive and the carceral as inbuilt in something which partakes of their nature without being necessarily associated with prisons: '*the disciplinary*' as the gist of modern civilization. That is why, in the end, his book speaks far more of discipline than of punishment. As a whole, therefore, *The Birth of the Prison* stands or falls with his unabashed *Kulturkritik* – the least convincing of its elements. For what Foucault offers can be considered a Marcusean account of the eighteenth century: a brazen historical caricature, where the Enlightenment features as an age of internalization of inhumanity, largely akin to that described by Marcuse as the essence of our own 'unidimensional' culture.

But Foucault's anathema, if not entirely original, had of course some novel ingredients. Two in particular are worth stressing. As a good (if unwilling) structuralist, Foucault refuses to see the evil – panopticism – as a simple effect of a given socio-economic infrastructure. Marx gets three or four references in *Discipline and Punish*. The most important is on page 221, where Foucault, in a long paragraph which is a masterpiece of theoretical equivocation, states at the same time: (a) that in the economic take-off of the West, the accumulation of men by dint of disciplinary methods and the accumulation of capital studied by Marx 'cannot be separated'; (b) that the growth of capitalism gave rise to disciplinary power, yet the techniques of the latter 'could be operated in the most diverse régimes'; (c) that the 'massive projection of military methods on to industrial organization' was 'an example' of the influence of disciplinary 'schemata of power' on the capitalist division of labour.

In other words, you can have it as you like it; but obviously Foucault would rather have his own *gauchisme* free of the stumbling block of economic or technoeconomic determinism. His alternative proposal, as a materialist, is, as the historian Jacques Léonard has perceptively noted,[20] the *focus on the body*. *Discipline and Punish* could in fact be called the first sustained attempt at offering a genealogy (a Nietzschean reduction of forms of action or knowledge to will-to-power configurations) in strongly *somatic* terms. Foucault is explicit about it: his aim was to tell the political history of the body.

But also of the soul. He regards his 'microphysics of punitive power' as an important element in the genealogy of the modern 'soul'.[21] Polemicizing against crass materialism, he argues that it is patently wrong to dismiss the soul as an illusion or an ideological effect. On the contrary, it very much exists – it is permanently produced on those punished, supervised, corrected and controlled. The soul, born of discipline and constraint, is both 'the effect and instrument of a political anatomy; the soul is the prison of the body'.[22] The ancient Gnostics' favourite pun was: *soma sema*, the body-tomb (of the soul). Foucault, the *libertin* anarchist – a nice pendant to Barthes, the anarchist *libertin* – overturns it: in carceral society, it is the soul which imprisons the body. Our freedom is our bodily life, uncolonized by social disciplines. There was a moment when Foucault was not too far from the 'desiring machines' of another neo-Nietzschean, Gilles Deleuze (*Anti-Oedipus*, 1972).

This focus on society-made 'souls' (which he equates with psyche, consciousness, subjectivity, personality, individuality, conscience and all their kith and kin) reasserts Foucault's culturalism at the heart of his political radicalism. *Discipline and Punish* came out when its author had already proved himself a militant prison-reformer and a theorist basically sympathetic to *gauchiste* rebellion as it exploded in 1968. Yet in his way of staying on the left of the left, he managed to keep a Nietzschean perspective; for all his libertine overtones, there is nothing 'naturist' in Foucault: no natural man, no *bon sauvage* is presupposed by his criticism of disciplinary culture. Unlike Marcuse, Foucault does not wage his *Kulturkritik* war in the name of natural instincts. Here lies the big difference between romantic and Nietzschean counter-Enlightenments – and the first main novelty in Foucault's cultural critique.

The second original point is his concern with knowledge, now in the guise of power/knowledge. Listen to him: 'We should admit [...] that power produces knowledge (and not simply by encouraging it because it serves power or by applying it because it is useful); that power and knowledge directly imply one another; that there is no power relation without the correlative constitution of a field knowledge, nor any knowledge that does not presuppose and constitute at the same time power relations.'[23] Again, this is, of course, a very Nietzschean thing to say. When all is told, then, one can say that Foucault is applying the lesson of Nietzsche to something made familiar to us by the general thrust of so-called Western Marxism (chiefly the Marxism of Lukàcs and of the older Frankfurt school): the conflation, that is, of social criticism (i.e., the indictment of bourgeois society) and a countercultural stance (the Great Refusal of modern civilization). On closer inspection, however, the picture is less simple. Nietzsche and the old Nietzscheans (e.g., Spengler) attacked modern culture as decadent. The new Nietzscheans in France, marked as they are by the impact of Marxism, attack it as repressive. What defined modern culture for Nietzsche was its lack of vitality; what characterizes it for Foucault – as for Adorno or Marcuse – is coercion. Foucault, like the Marxists, takes the side of the victims – a most un-Nietzschean position. Moreover, Nietzsche did not dislike the Enlightenment – far from it. In at least three books, *Human, All-Too-Human* (1878), *Dawn* (1881) and *The Joyous Science* (1882), he paid homage to its critical spirit. Foucault, on the other hand, turned out in *Discipline and Punish* as a fierce foe of the Enlightenment, resuming the hostility shown to it in *Madness and Civilization* (while *Les Mots et les choses*, no doubt because it handled the classical age *en bloc*, sounds far more neutral).

Thus at bottom Foucault follows Nietzsche in his view of reality (there is not truth, there are only interpretations) *but not in his view of history*. Or rather, what he borrows from Nietzsche, as far as history is concerned, is just a *formal* perspective: genealogy, namely, the problem of the emergence and descent of cultural phenomena. In genealogy, old cultural forms receive new functions, like the lazar houses transformed into asylums or the monastic cells converted into prison cages. Genealogy casts light on the pragmatism of history, on the human capacity to pour new wine into old cultural bottles. And it sees it all, of course, *from the viewpoint of power*, with truth debased to the role of an aid – or a mask – of domination.

Read as a Nietzschean or Marxo-Nietzschean countercultural manifesto, *Discipline and Punish* makes engrossing partisan history; but how does it read as history *tout court*? Let us turn to the historians' judgement. Take a recent, well researched work on executions and the evolution of repression: *The Spectacle of Suffering* by Pieter Spierenburg, of Erasmus University in Rotterdam. Following Norbert Elias's pioneering way of correlating moral and institutional changes, Spierenburg states (p. viii) that Foucault does not inquire into the translation from one penal system into another, does not explain the changes in modes of repression by relating them to other social developments and does not base his analysis of public executions on archival sources. Flatly warning that 'the infliction of pain and the public character of punishment did not disappear overnight', he reckons 'Foucault's picture [...] actually far from historical reality' (ibid). Lack of archival support is particularly conspicuous, according to Spierenburg (p. 108), in Foucault's thesis about the 'political danger' inherent in public executions, the danger of rioting beyond control, which he deems the cause of their eventual disappearance.

More generally, from a critical historiographic viewpoint, *Discipline and Punish* seems flawed on three scores. First, Foucault seems to get some of his most important facts wrong. Historians have complained, for instance, that the whole revolutionary period is largely absent from Foucault's story. Maybe he was too uncompromising in his (structuralist) distaste for the history of events (despite his flirtation with that notion in *The Archaeology of Knowledge*); but be that as it may, his silence on the French Revolution as a specific phase in penal history led him to overlook its role in key changes. As Léonard recalls, the revulsion against bloodshed after the Terror provided a major psychological push to the substitution of incarceration for the 'spectacle of the scaffold' (Alan Sheridan's felicitous English for Foucault's '*éclat du supplice*'). On the other hand, Napoleon's penal code of 1810, while improving on the detention system enacted by the revolutionary assemblies, re-established shameful punishments such as branding, the carcan or even the amputation at the wrist – these cruel penalties were not abolished until the July Monarchy.

I happen to own a poster which was designed to make public a judgement of the assizes of the Département du Nord from the summer of 1813, sentencing one François Mouquet, a worker, to five years' imprisonment plus the costs of the trial and one hour of carcan at the main square of Douai. Poor Mouquet's heinous crime boiled down to – as the poster says in high lettering – the theft of two handkerchiefs from a pub! The episode, showing as it does the ferocity of bourgeois penalty at the time – the eve of Victor Hugo's immortal Jean Valjean in *Les Misérables* – stresses two aspects minimized in

Discipline and Punish: the long afterlife of Ancien Régime penal elements in what Foucault presents as a clear-cut post-traditional 'disciplinary society', and the concrete evolution of class justice (as distinct from the largely undifferentiated bourgeois order the book alludes to).

Léonard puts his finger on at least three further omissions. First, Foucault does not distinguish between different categories of prisoners (political prisoners, murderers, workers, recalcitrant military, prostitutes, etc.), any more than he undertakes a sociology of judges and lawyers. Secondly, Foucault overstates the actual effects of 'normalization' in French society during the first half of the last century. The historian of the army, the historian of education and the historian of medicine can hardly buy Foucault's picture of an all-pervasive discipline: they are too much aware of the resistance of old customs and of the frequent impotence of so many regulations. Again, research in the history of work tends seriously to qualify Foucault's 'Taylorist' description of normalized industrial activity: France was still overwhelmingly a peasant and craft economy, and took a long time before adopting a full splitting of industrial tasks within factories. Finally, it may be argued, Foucault does not stress enough the religious origin and motivation of many a technique of drill or rite of exclusion belonging to his catalogue of disciplines.[24]

At this stage I feel tempted to add another possible bone of contention: the history of pedagogical thought. I could find no quotes from the *Emile* or from Pestalozzi in *Discipline and Punish*. Yet, as everyone knows, the late eighteenth century was an age of pedagogical effervescence, predominantly in an emancipatory and humanitarian direction. One of Foucault's footnotes refers to the scholarly work of G. Snyders, *La Pédagogie en France aux XVIIe. et XVIIIe. siècles* (1965). But he makes no use whatsoever of Snyders's well documented contrast between a 'pedagogy of surveillance' prevalent during the seventeenth century and the new, 'natural' teaching and learning methods gradually risen throughout the age of Enlightenment. If – just for the sake of argument – we accept the description of the bourgeois school as a mirror of the prison, then at the very least it should be mentioned that this 'carceral' education belied, instead of fulfilling, a good deal of the thought of the Enlightenment in matters educational.

A second major flaw in *Discipline and Punish* refers less to getting facts wrong than to lop-sided evaluations of historical data. Here the main casualty is the view of Enlightenment reformism. We saw how Foucault interprets it: as a totalitarian enterprise in all but name. However, this does not chime with the historians' appraisal – and I don't mean by it anything like naïve progressivist accounts. Take, for example, Franco Venturi, who after a lifetime of path-breaking research on the age of the Enlightenment had just published, a few years before Foucault's birth-of-the-prison book, a splendid work, *Settecento riformatore: da Muratori a Beccaria* (1969).

Cesare Beccaria, often called the father of penology, is unanimously deemed the key figure in enlightened penal reformism. His famous treatise *Dei delitti e delle pene* (Of Crimes and Punishments), published in 1765 when the author was still under thirty, and hailed by Voltaire and most of his fellow *philosophes*, commanded the field throughout Europe well into the next century. Accordingly, Foucault quotes it half a dozen times. Now when Professor Venturi delivered the George Macaulay Trevelyan lectures in Cambridge (subsequently published as *Utopia and Reform in the Enlightenment*, 1971) he chose to study the question of enlightened reformism from the viewpoint of 'the right to punish'. Inevitably, he centred his chapter on the European reception of Beccaria's ideas. Yet if we bear his analysis in mind we shall soon realize that something is amiss in the Foucaldian portrait of eighteenth-century penal ideology.

Venturi does not dream of concealing the occasional nasty streaks in the Enlightenment's social fantasy. He mentions, for instance, a modest proposal of the Abbé Morellet to transform convicts into true slaves who, as such, would be employed to procreate, with two advantages: adding to the labour force, and refuting prejudices about 'hereditary' vices. ... Beccaria himself was not above recommending the harshness of hard labour. In the drawing he sketched to illustrate the third edition (in just one year!) of his work, he put a Justice posing as Minerva (law and wisdom); but while the Justice-Minerva averts her horrified eyes from the heads the executioner is offering her, she turns a smiling gaze on several tools of hard labour: shovels, saws and their like. Nevertheless, Beccaria was far from envisaging the disciplinary activism, the meddling authorities, high and low, of Foucault's carceral society. He believed that jurists and legislators 'should rule the lives and fortunes of men tremblingly'. Venturi recalls that it was with regard to him that the word 'socialist' was first used in a modern language. '*Socialista*', in Latin, had been used by a German Benedictine, Anselm Desing, to denote natural law theorists like Pufendorf, who placed the *socialitas* or human social instinct at the basis of natural law. But when Ferdinando Facchinei – a staunch critic of Beccaria – employed the word in Italian in 1765, it had a quite different meaning: it meant an author wanting a society of free and equal men[25] (it was, of course, only much later – outside the purview of Venturi's study – that, among the left Saint-Simonians, socialism, the noun, was coined, in connection with the idea of a central regulation of the economy). The point, however, is that the chief penal reformer was an egalitarian libertarian; therefore, one can hardly take the Enlightenment's view of penalty as a gruesome disciplinary persuasion. Diderot thought Beccaria's plans were just an ineffectual Utopia (in fact, many of them were readily implemented, especially in the Austrian Empire's lands, though not in France). D'Alembert praised the profound humanity of Beccarian penology. Paradoxically, by restricting his handful of quotations to the utilitarian side of *Dei delitti e delle pene*, Foucault sides with those who, like Voltaire, strove to give a strictly 'technical', non-sociological (let alone 'socialist') interpretation of such a seminal and influential book. Yet Beccaria's utilitarianism, strong enough to place him among the main acknowledged forerunners of Bentham, was not at all incompatible (nor was Bentham's, for that matter) with powerful libertarian and philanthropic lines of thought. As Venturi recognizes, in practice, most plans for penal reform at the close of the eighteenth century exhibited a mixture of humanitarianism, economic calculation and remnants of ancient cruelty transmitted into new, more rational forms.[26] But not for a moment does he, or any other renowned historian of that age, suggest that the Enlightenment is best equated with a crippling overall disciplinary drive.

Lastly, a third kind of flaw in *Discipline and Punish* as a work of history lies in the nature of the *explanations* it offers. For instance, one of Foucault's central purposes is to show why imprisonment in penitentiaries came to be universally adopted in such a short time. Incarceration, after all, had been discarded by several penal reformers; how come it triumphed so quickly everywhere? Foucault's answer is twofold. He claims that (a) the disciplinary prison made its inmates into a useful working force, and (b) in any event similar disciplining institutions were already at work in other areas (the armed forces, the factory, the hospital, the school). Answer (a) blames class control on the rising bourgeoisie; answer (b) blames 'carceral society' on modern culture as a whole, embodied in the Enlightenment. Now the trouble is, if the prison springs from class domination, it should be explained how it came into force, almost simultaneously, in countries with widely different class structures.[27] Why, in particular, did it first appear in late eighteenth- and early nineteenth-century America, where obviously class conflict was far less bitter and widespread than in Europe? On the other hand, in Robert Brown's apt remark, Foucault, in describing the 'carceral' system, gives no account of its introduction into different institutional areas and especially into those which – like the school or the factory – do not normally constitute 'total institutions' in Erving Goffman's sense, i.e., are not in principle spaces cut off from the wider society. Critics like Brown are quite prepared to grant that ultimately Foucault is not engaged in an explanatory task. But then, they retort, neither should he ask the kind of questions he does ask about the expansion of disciplinary patterns in modern society.

At any rate, historical accuracy apart, Foucault's explanations are in themselves vitiated. As Karel Williams shrewdly observed, his kind of analysis tends constantly to be circular; its conclusions are already present at the beginning.[28] In other words, the method is eminently question-begging. Jon Elster has shown that Foucault slips into that 'obsessional' search for meaning' which often underpins pseudo-explanations couched in terms of consequences. According to Elster, one of the roots of the search for meaning at all costs is theological, and can be found in Leibniz' theodicy, the gist of which is the claim that evil and pain ought to be regarded as necessary causal conditions for the best of all possible worlds. When, for example, the functionalist school in the sociological theory of conflict states that conflict within and between bureaucratic structures shores them up against ritualism and sclerosis, we have the same kind of faulty argument from consequences. Now Foucault, as indicated, says that we should stop wondering at the failure of prison to deter crime and correct criminals and realize that the actual purpose of prisons is precisely to maintain and produce delinquency, by implicitly encouraging recidivism and converting the occasional offender into a habitual criminal. Although Foucault's rhetorical style leaves the consequence-explanation suggested rather than asserted, his reasoning entails the presumption that a *cui bono* question – what are prisons useful for? – is not just a heuristic guide among others, but a privileged path for reaching the true *raison d'être* of prisons.[29] The point is, teleological explanations of this kind do not, of course, qualify as genuine causal analysis; they just *assume* causes without demonstrating any causal mechanism; hence the circularity and the question-begging.

Notoriously, Foucault does not dress his teleological explanations in terms of agency. But neither does he discard altogether the possibility of planned action. More than one critic has noticed his large use of pronominal verbs, of the vague pronoun 'on' and other verbal devices whereby he avoids specifically imputing social processes to any humans, yet does not rule it out altogether. Léonard's comment hits the nail on its head: 'One does not know for certain whether M. Foucault describes a machinery or a machination.[30] Towards the end of *Discipline and Punish* 'the carceral' or 'the carceral archipelago' (doubtless an echo of Solzhenitsyn) recurs in a personalized way. Such prosopopoeias are the nemesis of an inveterate structuralist foible: the avoidance of analysis through action and intention. The dismissal of agency is felt to be mandatory, out of fear of falling into subject metaphysics (as though the two went necessarily together). Strictly speaking, however, in the *gauchiste* Foucaldianism of 1975, agency is at once dodged and undenied – a sop, as it were, to the radicals' taste for conspiracy theories of history.

8. Foucault's 'cratology': his theory of power

On the very last page of *Discipline and Punish* Foucault stresses that the 'the power of normalization' is not exercised by the prison alone, but also by our social mechanisms to procure health, knowledge and comfort. Consequently, adds he, 'the fabrication of the disciplinary individual' does not rest only on institutions of repression, rejection and marginalization. The carceral transcends the gaol. The study of the prison, therefore, was bound to unfold into an anatomy of social power at large – as well as, inevitably, a reconsideration of our very concept of power. No wonder so many of Foucault's texts and interviews since the mid-seventies expatiate upon the problem of modern forms of domination.

By searching for a genealogy of the modern subject, Foucault was automatically defining an angle where knowledge is enmeshed with power. Thus his pursuit of the modern subject through forms of knowledge as well as practices and discourses had to concentrate on what he calls *power-knowledge* (*pouvoir-savoir*), a Nietzschean perspective where all will to truth is already a will-to-power. And the more he delved into spheres of practical knowledge on the subject, the more he found *technologies of the self* waiting for analysis. At the end of the day, as Colin Gordon notes, Foucault developed a concept of power 'as able to take the form of a subjectification as well as of an objectification'.[1] The self as a tool of power, a product of domination, rather than as an instrument of personal freedom – this became Foucault's main theme after *Discipline and Punish*.

As already indicated, all this problematic presupposed a recasting of the concept of power. Put in a nutshell, it required a theory of *productive power*. The theory of discursive practices in *The Archaeology of Knowledge* and *L'Ordre du discours* remained tied up with too negative a view of power, stressing coercion, prohibition and exclusion. Since *Discipline and Punish* Foucault changed the focus. Now he warned: 'we must cease once and for all to describe the effects of power in negative terms: it "excludes", it "represses", it "censors", it "abstracts", it "masks", it "conceals". In fact, power produces; it produces reality; it produces domains of objects and rituals of truth. The individual and the knowledge that may be gained of him belong to this production.'[2]

Foucault buttresses his argument against repressive theories of power by a rhetorical question whose logical structure is analogous to his teleological pseudo-explanation of the survival of prisons despite their failure to deter crime: if power is indeed merely repressive, he asks, then how come power relations are not much more unstable than they are? Translation: the cause of power is its capacity to do something other than repress, just as the cause of the survival of the prison is its capacity to do something other than fail to prevent crime.

In 'The Subject and Power' (published as an afterword to Dreyfus and Rabinow's book on him) Foucault stated his aim: he wanted to study the 'how' of power, not in the sense of 'how does it manifest itself?' but of 'by what means is it exercised?' But much of what he added to this was commonplace to those familiar with the analytical literature on power from Weber to several contemporary philosophers, political scientists and sociologists. For instance, Foucault 'discloses', rather sententiously, that power properly speaking is really *over others*, *not over things* – it is a matter of domination, not of capacity. He also takes pains to stress that power acts upon our actions, not – as sheer physical violence – upon our bodies. 'Power is exercised only over free subjects and only insofar as they are free.' We stand enlightened. In the language of Roman law: *coactus tamen voluit*, i.e., coercion implies freedom. This slightly pompous exercise in elementary definitions boils down to something familiar yet rather tiresome: how often does radical thought, whenever it bothers to exchange rhetoric for reflection, discover long-found Americas!...

Foucault gets more interesting as he states that the exercise of power, being neither violence nor consent, is 'a total structure of actions brought to bear upon possible actions', inciting, seducing or, 'in the extreme', constraining and forbidding.[3] More interesting, but also considerably hazy: for how are we, in operative analytical terms, to equate power with a 'total structure of actions'? We can see where Foucault is sailing to: the old Marxist ghost of a 'power structure' feeding on a hypostatized set of class interests. But then he should choose: for either you analyse power in action terms or you conjure up such totalities. What you cannot do is to have your cake and eat it. Please note that I am not saying that you can't do class analysis, or study power in relation to class; all that is forbidden, if you care for analysis instead of sloganizing, is to pretend you are marching towards analysis with bluntly unspecified (and possibly unspecifiable) 'total structures of action'. For to begin with, if such concepts could ever be of use, then it would obviously be in theories holding that power 'manifests itself', *not* in theories concerned with rationally showing *by what means* it is actually wielded – and we saw Foucault discard the former.

The two lectures of January 1976 first published (in Italian) in the collection *Microphysics of Power* (1977) are, on some scores, far more rewarding. Foucault distinguishes between a number of theories of power. There is the 'economic' theory, found in liberalism as well as Marxism. It sees power as something one is able to possess or alienate like a commodity, the basic assumption here being that social power follows the model of a legal transaction involving contractual exchange (the liberal, or 'juridical' version) or alternatively, that power is a function of class domination resting on the control of economic factors (the Marxist version). Then there is a 'non-economic' theory. It asserts that power is not primarily the analogon of wealth, working for the reproduction of economic relations. Rather, it is 'above all a relation of force'. This was the view of Hegel, Freud and Wilhelm Reich. We have already indicated why Foucault finds fault with this repression theory of power. Finally, a third position envisages power not in economic or repressive terms, but *as war*. 'Power', states Foucault, 'is war, a war continued by other means,' to reverse Clausewitz's famous dictum. More precisely, power, within a given society, is 'unspoken warfare': it is a silent, secret civil war that re-inscribes conflict in various 'social institutions, in economic inequalities, in language, in the bodies themselves of each and every one of us'.[4]

Ultimately, however, Foucault declares the two non-economic views of power – the repression theory, or Reich hypothesis, and the war theory, which he ascribes to Nietzsche – as compatible and even 'linked'. He invites us to regard repression as 'the realization, within the continual warfare of this pseudo-peace (i.e., the normal state of society), of a perpetual relationship of force'.[5] Repression, therefore, is, after all, real – but just as a subordinate effect of power. Apparently, then, power both 'produces' and 'represses' – but it 'produces' before repressing, mainly because what it represses – individuals – are already, to a large extent, its 'products'.

The lectures of 'Microphysics of Power' were delivered in Italy in early 1976. One year later, interviewed by Lucette Finas for *La Quinzaine Littéraire*, on the publication of the first volume of his *History of Sexuality*, Foucault was saying this: 'I believe that power does not build itself by means of wills (individual or collective), nor does it stem from interests. Power builds and works by means of powers, of a host of issues and effects of power.'[6] A few weeks later, he told *Le Nouvel Observateur* that he sought 'elementary power relations' underpinning economic relations; he pursued power in its 'infra-state' level.[7] In the chapter on method in volume 1 of the *History of Sexuality* Foucault holds power 'omnipresent', not, he explains, 'because it englobes everything, but because it comes from everywhere'.[8]

Here we seem to have two problems conflated. On the one hand (a), by proclaiming the ubiquity of power, he appears to be asserting no more than the plausible idea that power is spread out across most areas of society, power relations obtaining, of course, in practically all spheres of life. On the other hand (b), Foucault exempts power from action analysis (no will, no intention, no interest will ever help us to understand power). However, (b) by no means follows from (a). The recognition that power may indeed be everywhere does not at all enjoin us to get rid of intentions and interests while studying it. A bad piece of structuralist subject-phobia has been yoked together with a sound promise of social power analysis.

In fairness to Foucault, it should be added that sometimes (and then, in his comments on his kind of analysis, not in his historical studies) he manages to make some truly empirical sense of all this talk against the subject. Getting down to the brass tacks of specific, well-documented situations, he claims that interpretations in terms of subjective meaning, interest and intention are not in such cases applicable. In a 1977 text included in *Power/Knowledge* ('The confession of the flesh'), he gives as an example of such situations the emergence in France, from 1825 to 1830, of strategies for fixing workers in the first French heavy industries at their workplaces. At Mulhouse and in the North, working people were pressed to marry; *cités ouvrières* were built; credit schemes devised to ensure advance payment of rents; a truck-system with grocers and wine-shops established; in sum, everything was attempted to retain the worker in a decent routine of labour and life. Now these strategies got a considerable reinforcement from originally entirely different initiatives, such as philanthropic moves to help and morally improve the toiling classes or governmental measures extending the school network; so the pursuit of different objectives added up to a pattern of workers' subjection. Another example: since the birth of modern prison, magistrates have often had to make room for psychiatric expertise, because the change in the 'humane' assumptions of the modern punitive régime made it inevitable. Once again, a complex pattern of domination evolved without its being possible for us to locate a definite group of actors willing it in a clear intentional way.

Foucault's point is that in such cases the historian faces 'strategic necessities which are not exactly interests'; at the end of the day, one gets complex but 'coherent, rational' global strategies, but it is no longer possible to identify the person, or persons, who conceived them. Nevertheless, it is not easy to see why we should so describe the situation. What seems clear is that there are multiple, convergent (as well as occasionally divergent) interests and intentions at work. But it doesn't follow that an analysis based on agency and interest is impossible. On the contrary: in order to understand what is or was going on, we still have to try to grasp what each actor or group of actors intended when they did this or that; we still need to interpret the entrepreneurs' plans, the philanthropists' campaigns, the magistrates' goals and so on. Interest-fuelled agency is there all the time, even at cross-purposes. All you surely don't have is One Big Subject – The Bourgeoisie, acting, just like a new Hegelian *Weltgeist*, behind the backs of real men differently engaged. Yet the empirical-minded social scientist never looked for such an uncanny entity in the first place. Monolithic class analysis of such coarseness has always been of very little use in social science, as opposed to political ideology. The many different subjects, individual and 'collective', are quite enough for the explanation of such social processes to get its teeth into. Therefore, the numerous empirical instances of complex social action unfolding in time (often with a lot of side-effects and unintended outcomes) is no grist to the mill of the *a priori* utter dismissal of the subject.

Fortunately, in a later text (the already quoted 'The Subject and Power') the belated discovery that power is exercised over free subjects seems to give the lie to reckless statements such as 'individuals are the vehicles of power, not its point of application [...] the individual is an effect of power'.[9] The true interest of *Microphysics of Power* lies in another direction: it lies in its attempt to sketch out a macrohistory of power. These lectures resume, on a more general level, the ideas of *Discipline and Punish* on the evolution of power systems.

In 'feudal' society, says Foucault, power was chiefly sovereignty and confined to 'general mechanisms' of domination; power had then 'little hold on detail'. But the classical age invented new mechanisms of power, endowed with 'highly specific procedural techniques' as well as new instruments and apparatuses. A new type of power – disciplinary domination – became 'one of the great inventions of bourgeois society'. Unlike random sovereign power, which was chiefly exercised 'over the earth and its products', disciplinary power concentrated on 'human bodies and their operations'. So, instead of discontinuous levies, modern man got constant surveillance.[10] Carceral society was born. And in view of this new configuration of power, this modern 'cratic' pattern, Foucault exhorts us to conduct 'an *ascending* analysis of power', starting 'from its infinitesimal mechanisms' in the manifold culture of modern societies. To chart power not from its 'higher' centre ('descending analysis') but from its humble ground and periphery – such was Foucault's programme in the seventies. It implied, as he put it, a sense of power in its 'more "regional" and local forms', down to its minute instances at its extremities, at those points where power becomes 'capillary'.[11]

Not only is modern power ubiquitous; it is also anonymous and comprehensive. It makes cogs in its machinery of us all, high and low, ruling and ruled. In his preface to a French edition of Bentham's *Panopticon*, entitled 'The Eye of Power' (1977), Foucault writes it in full: the characteristic of the societies installed in the nineteenth century is power as 'a machine in which everyone is caught, those who exercise [it] just as much as those over whom it is exercised'.[12] The trouble with Foucaldian epistemes, it may be remembered, was that they did seem monoliths. Is Foucaldian power, a 'total structure of action', also a monolith? The valiant Marxifying Foucaldian, Colin Gordon, is adamant: no, it isn't. He is aware that readers of Foucault often get the impression of 'a paranoid hyper-rationalist system in which the strategies–technologies–programmes of power merge into a monolithic régime of social subjection'. Yet it is all a terrible misunderstanding, for 'Foucault distinguishes his characterization of our societies as *disciplinary* from the fantasy of a *disciplined* society populated by docile, obedient, normalized subjects'. Gordon strives to prevent Foucault's assertion of an omnipresence of power from being misconstrued as though it amounted to an omnipotence of the modern apparatuses of domination.[13]

There are in fact some disclaimers in Foucault's own texts to this effect. Just the same, the latter also abound in holistic phrases, as several of our quotations have shown. How can readers avoid the impression of an omnivorous power monolith when, for each sporadic reassuring clause granting that power does not embrace everything, they stumble over scores of totalist expressions such as 'disciplinary society', 'disciplinary generalization', 'general tactics of subjection', 'generalized carceral system', 'carceral continuum', 'carceral texture of society', 'society of surveillance', and so on? How can they readily discard the idea of an omnipotent domination when they are told that our schools and hospitals and factories are essentially mirrors of the prison, our lives being everywhere 'normalized' from cradle to tomb? After all, if Foucault did not mean it, why the deuce did he keep saying it? How could so articulate a writer as he undoubtedly was be so awkward or so careless as to mislead his readers on such a vital point? Even if we admit that there may be an analysis waiting to be extracted from such a sweeping rhetoric of denunciation, we must as well acknowledge that while the analysis was never done, the rhetoric was overdone.

We can therefore say that one of the peculiarities of Foucault's anatomy of power is its *pancratism*: its tendency to sound as a systematic reduction of all social processes to largely unspecified patterns of domination. Now pancratism is a considerable liability from an analytical point of view. Indeed, to say that power is suffused all over society, or even that some form of power permeates all major social relations (two rather plausible propositions) does not mean that everything in society, or even everything significant therein, bears the imprint of power as a defining feature.

In legal philosophy, this has been realized by some critics of Kelsen. While the traditional position in legal theory held that coercion is the *instrument* of law, Hans Kelsen advanced the claim that the very *content* of law is the regulation of force. As he graphically put it (cf. *Reine Rechtslehre*, V, § 1), strictly speaking, we should never say that whoever commits an illegal act 'violates the law' – on the contrary, it is thanks to illicit acts that the law performs its essentially coercive task, which is to respond to illegal actions in the form of an effective sanction.

The trouble, as Alfonso Ruiz-Miguel saw, is that in order to equate the whole basic content of law with regulated force or coercion, one has to employ too wide a concept of power. Now, in principle, practically every social relation does lend itself to be seen in terms of power. For instance, we can very well interpret the legal demand that food products bear on a label the terminal date of their healthy use as proof of the power of consumers over producers, instead of regarding it as an impartial governmental regulation concerned with the prevention of diseases; or again, we can 'read' legal stipulations against illicit profit as evidence of the domination of honest businessmen over their naughtier trade-fellows. To this extent, a theory of power in society is virtually irrefutable – but by the same token, of little or no cognitive value. As Ruiz-Miguel wisely concludes, the result of thus reducing every social relation to power is descriptively very poor, since the overbroadening of the concept of power corresponds to an equal loss in depth and specificity.[14] Exactly the same drawback appears to afflict Foucault's description of social power. Jean Baudrillard said in *Oublier Foucault* (1977): 'Quand on parle tant du pouvoir, c'est qu'il n'est plus nulle part.' One might as well have it the other way round: the more you see power everywhere, the less you are able to speak thereof.

In a curious but understandable way, Foucault's political philosophy reflected his avoidance of human agency, as a corollary of the general structuralist dismissal of the subject. As Peter Dews has seen, Foucault purports 'to dissolve the philosophical link – inherited by the Marxist tradition from German idealism – between consciousness, self-reflection and freedom, and to deny that there remains any progressive political potential in the ideal of the autonomous subject'. For the subject/freedom link, Foucault substitutes 'a direct, unequivocal relation between subjectification and subjection'.[15] Foucault himself anyhow said that 'consciousness as the basis of subjectivity is a prerogative of the bourgeoisie'.[16] In his view, the politics of class struggle can and ought to be committed to a 'desubjectification' of the will-to-power.[17]

To the gulf between Foucault's views and the concept of freedom in German idealism one might add that he was not close to 'Western' (as distinct from German) ideas of liberty either. Roughly, we have had three main concepts of freedom historically active in modern political thought: the German idea of freedom (to borrow Leonard Krieger's label), based on reflection and *self-development*; the Lockean idea of liberty as *independence* and security, i.e., freedom from oppression and arbitrary interference; and the Rousseaunian idea of freedom as *autonomy* or self-determination. To the Germans (above all, Fichte and Hegel), freedom meant preeminently *inner* freedom; to Locke, its paramount meaning was *civil liberties*; and to

Rousseau, it meant primarily *political liberty*.

Now while Foucault's scorn of interests, in his analysis of power, left him without much use for the concept of freedom as personal independence, his conflation of subjectivity and subjection, besides undermining the notion of reflection as self-development, made a mockery of the idea of freedom as individual autonomy. As a consequence, Foucault had no room for the traditional recognition of basic differences between liberal regimes and despotic polities – a recognition shared with liberalism by mainstream radical thought, beginning with classical Marxism. Actually, Foucault set so little store by the gap between free and unfree civil societies that in 1976 he had the cheek to tell K.S. Karol in an interview on the Soviet penal system that the surveillance methods used in the USSR were just an enlarged version of disciplinary techniques first established by the Western bourgeoisie in the nineteenth century. 'Just as the Soviets adopted the principles of scientific management [...] they also adopted our disciplinary techniques, adding one new weapon, party discipline, to the arsenal we had perfected.'[18] There is something definitely perverse in so equating the Gulag with Taylorism as 'techniques easily transplanted'[19] and as such bequeathed by capitalism to Communist ideocracy. What the equation left out, in terms of historical analysis, was simply everything that counts – the whole ideological and institutional environment which, in the liberal West, never permitted the setting up and maintenance of Gulags, no matter how Western may have been (in fact, English), in its origins, the idea of small-scale concentration camps. Furthermore, this kind of historical howler is politically as dangerous as it is foolish. And let it not be said that Foucault was anyway plainly rejecting the Soviet system together with its allegedly borrowed disciplinary techniques. Condemning the Gulag is far from enough: one should do it without misconstruing its nature and ancestry. And the genealogist of modern power, of all people, should be the last to err in this respect.

The truth is, Foucault did not care much for the politics of liberty because he thought politics as such no longer mattered. Politics, in his view, was the child of Revolution. Speaking to *Le Nouvel Observateur* in 1977, he suggested that all revolution tends to deteriorate into Stalinism because it tends to be confiscated by the revolutionary state. Therefore revolutions have become highly undesirable. It follows that we are now living 'the end of politics'. For if it is true that genuine politics is an activity made possible by revolution, and revolution is no longer on, then politics must go.[20] Class struggle – which Foucault had no intention of dropping – must learn to circumvent the dead weight of politics.

Two months later he welcomed André Glucksmann's *The Master Thinkers*. A die-hard *gauchiste* among the *nouveaux philosophes*, Glucksmann eloquently if not cogently accused modern philosophy since Hegel of intellectual complicity in the violence of a history dominated by the principle of the revolutionary state.[21] In similar vein, Foucault's 'unpolitics' was a post-revolutionary radical activism which approved of the 'specific struggles against particularized power' of 'women, prisoners, conscripted soldiers, hospital patients and homosexuals'. At the same time, however, there was no question for him of being or becoming reformist: reform he held a 'stupid and hypocritical' notion.[22] One wonders why. The closest I came to an answer was when I discovered how Foucault would like to see his works function: 'I would like my books to be [...] Molotov cocktails, or minefields; I would like them to self-destruct after use, like fireworks.'[23]

Given Foucault's brilliant contribution to pyrotechnical philosophy, this sounds like a fine piece of stylistic self-knowledge. But the trouble is, printed Molotov cocktails can damage the ways we think about power and politics, not least by substituting fiery moods for cool rational analysis. For I can't help agreeing with Peter Dews: Foucaldian power, 'having nothing determinate to which it could be opposed, loses all explanatory content'.[24] The dogmatic elision of the subject robs coercion of its object, leaving domination dematerialized. As even an admirer, Edward Said, has rightly deplored, there was not a word about how and why power is conquered, employed or held on to.[25] Foucault's 'cratology' remains as unsatisfactory as his history of punishment and discipline.

9. Politics of the body, techniques of the soul: Foucault's history of sexuality

In Foucault's previous historical work, the self was seen chiefly as a tool of power; selfhood was normalized subjectivity. In *The History of Sexuality* the self remains a prey to power, but now the story of its production by power is told, as it were, *from the inside*. Consequently the foreground is no longer occupied by power structures or strategies, but by 'technologies of the self' envisaged in their own inner space. We may remember that, according to his own definition of his project, Foucault was indeed less concerned with power per se than with power *in the emergence of the modern subject*. Sexual history is above all a way of allowing the genealogy of the subject to return to the centre of the stage. 'When I was studying asylums, prisons and so on' – he wrote in 1981 – 'I perhaps insisted too much on the techniques of domination. [...] I would like, in the years to come, to study power relations starting from the techniques of the self.'[1]

The avowed goal of Foucault's *History of Sexuality* is to highlight the *discourse* of sex in relation to 'polymorphous techniques of power'. Not sex as practice, but sex as the theme of a manifold discursive practice, is the subject matter of what turned out to be his last historico-analytical enterprise. Like *Madness and Civilization* and *The Order of Things*, *The Will to Truth* starts its periodization at the Renaissance. Once again, however, the Renaissance is just a foil to the first important mutation discerned by Foucault: the change in Western attitudes towards sex. Since the mid-sixteenth century, Western culture began to develop new, powerful techniques for internalizing social norms related to morals and, in particular, to sexual behaviour. But these post-Renaissance developments were in turn a reinforcement and intensification of the medieval establishment of *confession* as a main ritual of truth-production. The codification of the sacrament of penance at the Lateran Council of 1215, the substitution of interrogation for ordeal, the setting up of tribunals of Inquisition – all were significant in this evolution, and reflected, furthermore, on the career of the word 'avowal' – a term which was once a mark of status granted to one person by another but ended up by denoting someone's acknowledgement of one's own actions and thoughts. With the Council of Trent (1545–63) new procedures were adopted to purify ecclesiastic personnel. Elaborate techniques of self-examination, confession and direction of conscience began to be used in seminaries and monasteries. Meanwhile, the laity were summoned to confess far more often than before. Up to the Tridentine Counter-reformation the Church supervised sexuality only from a distance, for the requirement of *annual* confessions was hardly suitable for a close inspection of sexual behaviour. Generally speaking, therefore, the mutation came by 1550: 'For a long time, the individual was vouched for by the reference to others and the demonstration of his ties to the commonweal (family, allegiance, protection); then he was authenticated by the discourse of truth he was obliged to pronounce concerning himself.'[2] In the social sphere, sexuality takes form as a historical figure when sex is severed from the realm of prescriptive alliance. It is emphatically an idea of sex connected with the emergence of the modern individual.

Western man was thus converted, in early modern times, into a practitioner in the art of scrutinizing sin as intention, as well as perusing troubled feelings bound to the flesh. In time, the confessional conduct became part and parcel of modern life – and proved able to survive the general secularization of culture.

The confession has spread its effects far and wide. It plays a part in justice, medicine, education, family relationships and love relationships, in the most ordinary affairs of everyday life, and in the most solemn rites; one confesses one's crimes, one's sins, one's thoughts and desires, one's illnesses and troubles. [...] One admits to oneself, in pleasure and in pain, things it would be impossible to tell anyone else, the things people write books about. [...] Western man has become a confessing animal.[3]

Moreover, since the eighteenth century, demographers and administrators started to study population, prostitution and the patterns of spread of disease. 'Sex was [no longer] something one simply judged; it was a thing one administered.'⁴ Since the dawn of the industrial age, Western civilization colonized our biology: it devised an *'anatomopolitics'* – a politics of the body – in conjunction with a *'biopolitics'* – the planning of the population. Human sciences such as psychology, medicine and demography seized on the 'confessed' body as an object of social concern and governmental manipulation. Once more, a crucial alliance between power and knowledge was struck.

But the point is that sexuality became the chief subject matter of a generalized thrust of truth about the individual which turned out to have an almost boundless potential for the social power strategies. Once detached from the clutches of sin, the 'confessing animal' went on laying bare his soul; he and the *homo docilis* of disciplinary society are ultimately twins. 'The obligation to confess is now [...] so deeply ingrained in us, that we no longer perceive it as the effect of a power which constrains us; on the contrary, it seems to us that truth, lodged in our most secret nature, "demands" only to surface.'⁵ Now 'sex' is the epitome of this soul-searching individuality. While the East created a sophisticated and impersonal *ars erotica*, modern Western culture developed a *scientia sexualis* more intent on personalized control than on skilled pleasure.

A footnote in *The Will to Truth* discloses the original plan of the multi-volume *History of Sexuality*: from volume 2 on, there would be concrete historical studies on the four main objects (or victims) of socio-sexual control: women (especially in the figure, so characteristic of the heyday of bourgeois morality, of the hysteric); children (especially in regard to masturbation); the perverse adult; and 'populations and races'. *The Will to Truth*, by contrast, purports to be primarily a methodological discussion. The central issue at stake is to ascertain whether the sexual misery of modernity is due to prohibitions dictated by economic exploitation – a 'Work, make not love' situation. Such was, in fact, the view of Reich and Marcuse; and it may be remembered that Reich reached it by historicizing Freud's idea of instinctual repression as the basis of civilization: to Reich, far from underpinning all human societies, repression was just a historical stage, peculiar to authoritarian societies. Modern Western culture was to his mind such a kind of society, where repression necessarily obtains on behalf of capitalist exploitation.

Foucault was unconvinced by such views. He did not deny the modern sexual misery but refused to explain it as an outcome of repression. Instead, he set out to identify 'positive mechanisms' which, by 'producing' sexuality in a given cultural mode, engender unhappiness. That control by 'productive' rather than repressive power is at work in modern sexuality is witnessed by the fact that (as Foucault stressed in an interview to Bernard-Henri Lévy) the powers that be no longer seem to fear sex.[6]

'Repression' cultural critics, well acquainted with Marcuse, would of course reply that this is so because we live in a world of 'repressive desublimations' so that Foucault's remarks on the speedy 'liberation' of sexual mores in advanced capitalism are of no avail as a refutation of repression theory. In my view, Foucault's own brand of *Kulturkritik* has, in this connection, the advantage of descriptive, if not explanatory, realism: unlike the Marcuseans, he at least called a spade a spade. Moreover, he is now supported by the latest historiographic research on bourgeois sex, even in Victorian times. Foucault, after all, did not deny Victorian puritanism; he just reckoned it a 'digression and diversion' in the plurisecular 'process of transforming sex into discourse'.[7] Now it so happens that Peter Gay, while chiding Foucault for his 'anecdotal' procedure, 'almost wholly unencumbered by facts', describes his own recently published *Education of the Senses* (the first instalment of a massive work, *The Bourgeois Experience*) as a 'long argument' against what Foucault dubs the 'repressive hypothesis'.[8] And as Gay's subtitle – 'Victoria to Freud' – indicates, his thesis is that *even in the nineteenth century* decorum and repression were, to a large extent, more of a myth than the massive reality they are thought to have been.

To Foucault, the modern control of sexuality in bourgeois culture was less a weapon for use against the lower classes than an instrument of bourgeois self-idealization. Just as the disciplinary techniques which arose with the birth of the prison were originally a means of controlling the working class, the discourse on sex emerged primarily as a technology of the self wielded by the bourgeois sculpting his own image. The bourgeoisie built a code of sex for its own self-assertion. It erected the heterosexual monogamous couple into the standard of morality and pillar of society. Every other form of sex came to be regarded as contrary to nature and dangerous to society. Yet in the end even this aspect of class culture turned out to be an episode in the great saga of sex '*mis en discours*'. Heretic sex also took its place in more than one of the 'spirals of power and pleasure' which Foucault describes: for 'productive' power is also quite capable of breeding pleasure as well, however inauthentic. At any rate, Foucault's strong culturalist position prevented him from ever opposing anything remotely like 'natural sex' to the figures of modern eroticism. To him discourse does not so much tame sex as it 'invents' it. Throughout *The Will to Truth*, sex is social rather than natural; and at the end of his introductory volume, Foucault made a point of warning us against putting sex on the side of reality and sexuality on the side of ideas as illusions. No: sex as discourse is an idea which is neither nature nor, by no means, an illusion: it is a *historical* reality. As he briefly and provocatively put it in an interview: 'We have had sexuality since the eighteenth century, and sex since the nineteenth. What we had before that was no doubt the flesh.'[9]

In the same interview ('The Confession of the Flesh') Foucault explained what he meant by a discourse on sexuality. We saw that in the Foucaldian sense 'discourse' always connotes power. Now Foucault insists on a related concept, 'the apparatus [*dispositif*] of sexuality'. The apparatus 'consists in strategies of relations of forces supporting, and supported by, types of knowledge'. Unlike epistemes, apparatuses are both discursive and non-discursive; and they are also 'much more heterogeneous'.[10] Apparatuses are motley ensembles made of discourses, institutions, laws, administrative measures, scientific statements, philanthropic initiatives, etc. Sexuality, possessing no well-defined institutional slots such as the prison, is a prize field for the intrinsic heterogeneity of such power/knowledge apparatuses.

The Will to Truth seems to complete an interesting departure from what, despite his constant disclaimers, put Foucault close to structuralism. If *Discipline and Punish* substantially attenuated caesuralism, *The History of Sexuality* simply brushes it aside. In a sense, the power theme overrides all archaeological considerations, and Foucault appears to have broken with break theory. Unlike the three-age tale of *Madness and Civilization* (Ship of Fools/Great Confinement/Age of Psychiatry), *Les Mots et les choses* (resemblance/representation/'anthropologism' epistemes) and *Discipline and Punish* (torture/penal reform/incarceration), *The Will to Truth* seems basically built on two periods: before and after the *mis en discours* of sex, the time before and the time since the confessional age. The break is there, but it is a single one and there is no fuss about it as such.

What is more, the succeeding volumes of the work, far from stressing the break in the days of early modern puritanism and Counter-reformation moralism, stretches the historical range much further back. In fact, instead of grappling, as promised, with the 'marginal' sexualities of the woman, the child and the perverse (or rather the Western discourse on them), volumes 2 and 3 of *The History of Sexuality*, as they came out in June 1984, take an unexpected path: they deal with attitudes towards sex in Antiquity, both pagan and palaeo-Christian. The brilliant last chapter in *The Will to Truth* had actually contrasted two cultural eras: long ago, a *blood society*, defined by a warrior's ethic, a fear of famine, and punishment as torture; nowadays, a *sex society*, the scientific culture of biopolitics and normalizing disciplines. Yet as early as 1981, Foucault was already disclosing a different genealogical pattern, harking back to the rise of Christianity in late Antiquity. Let's take a look at the new picture.

From the outset, *The History of Sexuality* purported to understand how, in modern Western culture, there emerged an *experience* of sexuality: the birth and growth of 'sex' and 'sexuality' as historically given cultural objects. Foucault did not want to undertake either the history of ideas on sex or a history of mentalities ('*histoire des mentalités*', a popular game among contemporary French historians, stemming from one of the leaders of the Annales school, Lucien Febvre); he wanted to stick to a historical analysis of a specific experience: *the self-awareness of the individual as subject of a sexuality*. As we saw, the rise of such an experience seemed to him a nineteenth-century phenomenon, roughly coincident with the modern, historical episteme, the psychiatrization of insanity, and the spread of the penitentiary – to quote his three previous major historiographic labours.

In the introduction to *L'Usage des plaisirs* – volume 2 in the new structure of *The History of Sexuality* – Foucault says that his original project aimed at correlating, within a given culture, 'fields of knowledge, types of normativity and forms of subjectivity', or rather, the different 'truth games' ('*jeux de vérité*') obtaining in each of these spheres. In addition, he suggests that whilst he had analysed the formation of knowledge correlated with power and subjectivity in studies like *Histoire de la folie*, as well as systems of power in a book such as *Discipline and Punish*, the perusal of the modes of *self*-recognition of 'sexual subjects' still lay ahead of him – hence the need for a Foucaldian history of 'desiring man' ('*l'homme de désir*').[11]

But why exactly *sex*? asks Foucault. Why is it that sensual pleasures and sexual activities are so often the object of such moral concern, far more than other, hardly less vital experiences, like feeding oneself? An answer springs to mind: because sex, much more than almost anything else, is also the object of fundamental prohibitions, whose transgression is considered deadly serious. Now Foucault thought this answer perfectly question-begging. For quite often the moral concern with sexuality is stronger where no obligation or prohibition regarding sex is in order. Instead of prohibitions, he sought to ground his search for the prehistory of the sexual subject on the early Western development of 'self-techniques' (*techniques de soi*), or (to say it with Plutarch) of the '*ethopoetical*' function. 'I was led' – says Foucault at the close of his introductory pages – 'to substitute a history of ethical problematics from the viewpoint of self-techniques for a history of moral systems from the viewpoint of prohibitions.'[12]

Hence the title, *L'Usage des plaisirs* – actually a felicitous borrowing from the hedonic terminology of classical Greek: *chresis aphrodision*, the use of pleasures. Choosing an 'archaeo-genealogical' approach, Foucault discusses, throughout tomes 2 and 3 of *The History of Sexuality*, documents of a certain nature: *prescriptive* ancient texts, that is to say, texts which, no matter what their form – dialogues, treatises, collections of precepts, letters – sought primarily to propose rules of (sexual) behaviour. Such texts acted as 'operators' enabling individuals to question their own conduct in order to build their own personalities – the very stuff of character-making, or 'ethopoetics'.

Foucault began by questioning some conventional wisdom about the differences between pagan and Christian culture. Where lies the main cleavage between the sexual morals of paganism and Christianity? Many would reply that while in Antiquity sex has a positive meaning, Christianity associated it with sin and evil; again, for Christians the sole legitimate sexual partners were the monogamous couple (and even so, only when intent on procreating), whereas the Ancients took a distinctly more liberal view and indeed accepted homosexual relationships, at least between men. In reality, however, ancient sexual ethics in the West were far less permissive and 'Dionysian'. They actually had gone a long way, well before the rise of Christianity, in attaching negative values to sex, let alone sexual licence. The ancient world extolled the monogamous couple as the correct model for love and begetting, and even praised chastity and continence. Moreover there was already a link between sexual abstention and the access to Truth, most notable in the Socratic teachings as reported by Plato.

Foucault illustrates this point with great skill. He quotes a curious passage from St Francis of Sales's *Introduction to the Devout Life* (1609):

I will tell you a point of the elephant's honesty. An elephant never changes his mate. He loves her tenderly. With her he couples not, but from three years to three years. And that only for five days, and so secretly that he is never seen in the act. But the sixth day, he shows himself abroad again, and the first thing he does is to go directly to some river and wash his body, not willing to return to his troupe of companions till he be purified. Be not these goodly and honest qualities in a beast by which he teaches married folk not to be given too much to sensual and carnal pleasures?

Nothing could sound more 'Christian' on sex, one would normally think. Yet in fact St Francis's typical text, so transparently Christian in its concern with chastity, is but a modern variation of a classical theme. Aldrovandi (whom we met in *Les Mots et les choses*) and others bequeathed it to Counter-reformation ideology; but it was in fact Pliny the Elder, the naturalist who died at the Vesuvius eruption of 79 AD, who was first impressed by such prude pachyderms (cf. his *Natural History*, VIII, 5, 13). Though he did not urge conjugal purity as a general rule, as St Francis was to do, Pliny wrote in patent approval of a model of sexual behaviour already much lauded by some philosophical sects of the time, such as the later Stoics. Countless other texts also show that the sexual views of learned Greeks and Romans were far from lewd. In more than one point, they rather prefigured Christian modesty and rigorism.

The big difference, according to Foucault, is that the austerity claims of the Ancients were not organized into a unified moral code imposed upon everybody. Rather, they were experienced as a kind of de luxe morals vis-à-vis current practices. Furthermore, these austerity claims and the main legal and religious prohibitions of the time did not overlap, as witnessed by the fact that the rigorist literature was not addressed to those who were placed under the harshest constraints: women. The reason for this is that there are at least three levels in the history of morals: the level of actual mores or *customs* (*moralités*); the level of the moral *codes* of a given society; and finally the manner in which individuals are urged to constitute themselves into subjects of moral conduct – the *ascetic* level. Now conscious moral thought among the Ancients seems to have been much more geared to asceticism in this sense than to moral codification. In sum: whenever the ancient world theorized on sex, it was by no means in a lenient permissive mood; and such theorization was by definition directed not to one and all (as the rules of a Christian or Muslim community) but just to the natural members of the ruling class: free males.[13]

L'Usage des plaisirs examines the way Greek philosophy and medical thought tackled the problem of sexual ethics in three different areas of experience: dietetics (the regime of the body), the economy (the management of the *oikos* or household), and courtship. The objects of sexual ethics were *ta aphrodisia*, 'the works of Aphrodite' (*erga Aphrodites*), in Latin 'venerea', in French (approximately) '*voluptés*'. Foucault set out to outline the general form taken by the moral reflection on such pleasures in several texts – mostly by Xenophon, Plato and Aristotle – forming a specific field of 'problematization': an erotic episteme, as it were.

For the Greek authors, immorality in sex lay in excess and passivity, not in the thing itself. Sex – too much sex – was viewed as a potential danger rather than as an intrinsic evil. Aulus Gellius attributed to Hippocrates the dictum that orgasms are small epileptic strokes; but Democritus, often named as one of Hippocrates' teachers, did not think otherwise. Anyhow, coitus was regarded as a kind of violent mechanics. The rubbing up of the genitalia, together with the movement of the whole body, led to a warmth and agitation which as a result made so fluid the 'spermatic humour' that it ended up by foaming (*aphrein*: to foam) 'like all shaken fluids', in Hippocrates' own words. The common root of *aphrein* and the *aphrodisia* was not, of course, overlooked; was not Aphrodite herself divinely born out of the waves' froth?

The problem of sexual ethics, then, boiled down to an exercise in control: worth, in sexual behaviour, was tantamount to self-restraint. Wisdom meant keeping desire as close as possible to physical need. Not surprisingly, the Cynics, among all philosophical sects, stood out as standard-bearers of this naturist outlook. One fine day Diogenes braved public morality by masturbating *au plein air*. Dion of Prusa recorded for us his rationale: such a gesture, said the laughing cynic, was a natural remedy, a simple, honest relief by which man did not become a hostage to the tyranny of unbridled desire. Made in time, it might even have avoided the Trojan war.... What a pity Paris was not a Cynic.

Above all, sex was regarded as a key test for *enkrateia*: literally, self-mastery. Plato's *Republic* (IV 430) defined temperance as a kind of 'order and control' imposed on pleasures and desires. Aristotle's *Nicomachean Ethics* stressed the agonist nature of *enkrateia*, a moral fight distinct as such from prudence or *sophrosyne*, the placid virtue by which one chooses one's acts according to cool reason. Encratic men triumph first and foremost over themselves; they know how to master their passions in order to steer a middle course between profligacy and insensitivity. Free men ought not be slaves of their own desire. Liberty begins at home, within the soul; encratic man is a king to himself (*basilikos heautou*). And *enkrateia*, of course, implied *askesis*: for, if virtue is a struggle, it can hardly be attained without a proper drill.

Thus the status of the master of the *oikos*, the free citizen in the polis, was reflected in the moral ideal of passion-mastery. But this warrior ethic applied to the psyche remained, as we saw, eminently a male affair. Most characteristically, when it comes to the third test area of the sexual ethic, beside dietetics and economy, namely, the regulation of courtship, it involved less men and women than men in love with men. Courtly love in Greece (though not in Rome) meant primarily the ethics of the pursuit of boys. Foucault has much to say on it.[14] He starts by noting that in Antiquity the man who preferred boys to women did not think of himself as a pervert. On the contrary, when, in the *Symposium*, Plato distinguished between two loves, the higher, 'celestial' eros addressed itself only to young men. What mattered, though, was the kind of love, not its object, man or woman. Greek writers poured contempt on easy ephebes and ridiculed queers, one of the laughing stocks of ancient comedy. There was a natural revulsion, not towards the man who loved boys or who when young had been loved by an older man, but towards trusting with any place of social prominence anyone who had let himself be just a sex object - for this went straight against the noble logic of *enkrateia*.

By the same token, there was a sharp distinction between the role of the *erastos* - the loving elder man - and that of the *eromene* - his beloved one. Eromenes were by no means supposed fully to respond to the wooing, let alone the sexual urge, of their lovers, since by so doing they would be promptly disqualified as future citizens. The eros of pederasty was conspicuously asymmetrical. Hence the concern in the literature with the complex psychology involved in the honour of boys - a preoccupation later transferred, in the Christian West, to the nubile girl or young wife, the new objects of courtly love and ethico-erotic disquisitions.

Eventually homosexual relations were expected to evolve, if not originate, as *philia* - virile friendship, divested of carnal aspects. At any rate, the Greeks looked down on outgrown homosexualism. Loving young men beyond adolescence did not enjoy moral legitimacy; therefore, eros should be wisely converted into a manly *philia*. At the same time, it was between man and boy, not husband and wife, that a socially reciprocal relation formed itself, outside institutional constraints. Whereas Greek wives had no acknowledged moral autonomy, boys and men whom they met in the palestra or the street were social equals. Consequently, whatever rules there were between them belonged to an existential aesthetics rather than to a collective moral code. Erotics was this: a stylization (Foucault's word) of conduct, leaving plenty of room for free action.

L'Usage des plaisirs closes with a long, thoughtful comment on how Plato, in the *Symposium* and the *Phaedrus*, changed an erotics modelled on courtship and the freedom of male lovers into an erotics hingeing upon 'an asceticism of the subject and a common access to truth'. Foucault beautifully wove his Platonic finale into the framework of his *Leitmotiv* - the ethics of eros, beyond all self-indulgence:

This philosophical reflection on boys contains a historical paradox. To such masculine love, and more precisely to this love for boys and adolescents, which later would be so long and so harshly condemned, the Greeks granted a legitimacy where we like to recognize the proof of their freedom in these things. Nevertheless, it was on this subject, much more than on health (though they also worried about it), much more than on women and marriage (though here, too, they took care to set everything in good order), that they claimed the strictest austerity. True, except occasionally, they have neither condemned nor forbidden it. However, it is in their reflections on the love of youngsters that we see them utter the principle of an 'indefinite abstention', the ideal of renunciation whose paradigm was given by Socrates, in his unflinching resistance to temptation, together with the theme that renunciation holds in itself a lofty spiritual value.[15]

To us moderns, it is a paradox to see in such deviant love 'the need for a tough combat... against oneself, the gradual purification of a love in search of the truth of being, as well as man's soul-searching as subject of desire'.[16]

In Plato, the erotics of classical Greek culture was at once sublated and sublimated. Not even in Plato, however, did Eros surrender its sensual spirit. Ultimately the classical mind never did sever sex and love from pleasure; the libido bore serious dangers, but was never seen as an alien power, hostile to man. Following instead of mastering it (or instead of obliging only when desire was the child of genuine need) meant self-enslavement; but it was not a stain, a sign of damnation. Would all that be modified in the Hellenistic age and, later on, in the golden decades of the Roman Empire? The question is answered in volume 3 of *The History of Sexuality*: *Le Souci de soi* (The Concern for Self).

'Le Souci de soi' translates the Socratic phrase *epimeleia heautou*, rendered as *cura sui* in Latin. Foucault's third volume traces it in the first two centuries AD. He detects - as compared with classical thought - a stronger distrust of pleasures, insisting that excesses are noxious to both body and soul; an enhanced appreciation of marriage and conjugality; and a clear withdrawal of the higher meanings once attached to pederasty. Generally speaking, there was no strengthening of moral codes, but an intensification of demands for austerity connected with further stress on the importance of self-control. From the age of Socrates, Democritus and Hippocrates to that of the late Antonines and their physician, Galen (131-201), Greek and Roman thinkers came greatly to value continence and even abstinence. Besides, they put more emphasis on the pathogenic power of sex; Foucault speaks of '*une certaine pathologisation*' of the coitus.[17] At the same time, philosophers raised a veritable paean to unselfish self-concern. The Stoics made it into an art, attested by the definition of man by Epictetus ('the being assigned to a concern for selfhood') and by countless verbs in Seneca's letters and treatises: *sibi vacare, se formare, se facere, sibi applicare, suum fieri, in se recedere, secum morari*, etc. Seneca gave also (in his *De ira*) the fullest description of a new, highly esteemed moral technique: self-examination (*examen de conscience*). One century later, Marcus Aurelius expatiated most cogently on self-knowledge and self-mastery. But Foucault is perhaps still more original and insightful in his remarks on practical-minded minor Roman Stoics such as Musonius Rufus, the eloquent advocate of marriage against the scorn of Cynics and Epicureans; and he is most engaging in his comments on Pliny's moving pages on a husband's absence on duty and his fervent love - both *eros* and *philia* - for the young wife he left in Rome. Even the first Western poetry of conjugal love, in the *Silvae* of Statius (45-96 AD), gets an apt quote.

Le Souci de soi does not overlook the extent to which social change during the Hellenistic age, and then in imperial Rome since the Augustan period, conditioned new trends in ancient erotics. Building on the work of classicists like Claude Vatin and Paul Veyne, Foucault noted that the institutionalization of marriage by mutual consent in post-classical Antiquity backed up the idea of a tender conjugality. The same basic evolution took place in Rome: in republican times, marriage was preeminently a matter of role-playing under a patriarchal regime; there was little room for feeling in it. In the Empire, by contrast, the law of the heart became functional. In both worlds, Greek and Roman, there arose a 'conjugalization' of sexual intercourse. The emergence of imperial patterns and the attendant taming of the nobility into a 'managerial aristocracy' (in Sir Ronald Syme's phrase) also contribute to the new awareness of selfhood: the new gap between birth and office entailed both status-seeking and a quest for self.

In Antiquity there was no dramatic discontinuity in the practice of aphrodisia; erotics, on the other hand, was sharply dualistic: it always opposed 'vulgar' to 'noble' love. Under Christianity it was the other way round: love became unitary (and, of course, 'de-hedonized'), whereas pleasure-practice was given a strict borderline, separating legitimate heterosexual intercourse from the illicit amours of homosexuality.[18] Nevertheless, the heyday of imperial Rome already saw the rise of a theoretical trend towards a unitary erotics. Thus in the *Dialogue on Love* by Hadrian's preceptor, Plutarch (who, significantly, also authored some *Conjugal Precepts*, where *eros* is firmly built into *gamos* or marriage), the dualism of classical erotics is rejected. Characteristically, the shift to a unified *eros* went together with a sharp disparagement of bisexual practices (unified *aphrodisia*). Plutarch launched a cogent attack on the hypocrisy of those who defended pederasty on lofty philosophical grounds, disguising as much as possible its carnal basis, as though Achilles had not wept over the memory of Patroclus's thighs... . Plutarch introduced a key concept: *charis*, the consent granted by a woman in love - and which, as we noticed, could not possibly be accorded by a young to an older man without morally disqualifying the former. Thus late pagan philosophy, like Christianity, unified the field of love theory; but unlike Christian thinkers, it did not cleave the ancient unity of love and sex, sentiment and pleasure.

In conclusion, Foucault recalled the early modern debate on the relation between Stoicism and Christianity. To Renaissance humanists like Justus Lipsius, Epictetus was a true Christian in all but the name. In the sterner opinion of a Jansenist like Arnauld he was no such thing: the Stoics were virtuous people, but no Christians. Foucault took his stand in Arnauld's camp. To him, for all its moralizing evolution, its overall shift to upholding an 'elephant paradigm' for sexual life, ancient thought kept at bay one crucial dimension: the confessional thrust of Christianity. Writing in the *London Review of Books* in 1981, when his two volumes on Antiquity were in the making, he drove this point home by stressing the key place of 'truth as a duty' in Christian culture. Here is the gist of it in two long but luminous paragraphs:

As everybody knows, Christianity is a confession. This means that Christianity belongs to a very special type of religion - those which impose obligations of truth on those who practise them. Such obligations in Christianity are numerous. For instance, there is the obligation to hold as truth a set of propositions which constitute dogma, the obligation to hold certain books as permanent sources of truth and obligations to accept the decisions of certain authorities in matters of truth. But Christianity requires another form of truth obligation. Everyone in Christianity has the duty to explore who he is, what is happening within himself, the faults he may have committed, the temptations to which he is exposed. Moreover everyone is obliged to tell these things to other people, and hence to bear witness against himself.

These two ensembles of obligation - those regarding the faith, the book, the dogma, and those regarding the self, the soul and the heart - are linked together. A Christian needs the light of faith when he wants to explore himself. Conversely, his access to the truth can't be conceived of without the purification of the soul. The Buddhist also has to go to the light and discover the truth about himself. But the relation between these two obligations is quite different in Buddhism and in Christianity. In Buddhism, it is the same type of enlightenment which leads you to discover what you are and what is the truth. In this simultaneous enlightenment of yourself and the truth, you discover that your self was only an illusion. I would like to underline that the Christian discovery of the self does not reveal the self as an illusion. It gives place to a task which can't be anything else but undefined. This task has two objectives. First, there is the task of clearing up all the illusions, temptations and seductions which can occur in the mind, and discovering the reality of what is going on within ourselves. Secondly, one has to get free from any attachment to this self, not because the self is an illusion, but because the self is much too real. The more we discover the truth about ourselves, the more we have to renounce ourselves; and the more we want to renounce ourselves, the more we need to bring to light the reality of ourselves. That is what we could call the spiral of truth formulation and reality renouncement which is at the heart of Christian techniques of the self.[19]

By contrast, ancient moral reflection on pleasures was 'geared neither to a codification of acts nor to a hermeneutic of the subject but to a

stylization of attitude and an aesthetics of existence'.[20] In short: it
was an *art de vivre*, lost with the triumph of salvation-anxiety.

Foucault found a telling evidence of this change from *ars erotica*
into confessional control in the contrast between the pagan approach
to the interpretation of dreams and the way St Augustine considers
sex. *Le Souci de soi* dwells on the *Oneirocritica* of Artemidorus of
Ephesus, who lived in the second century AD.[21] Artemidorus was the
anti-Freud: in his four chapters on sexual dreams, he took sex as the
signifier of portents to come, instead of holding the sexual as the
ultimate 'signified' of dream images. Also, he saw dreamed sexual
acts as harbingers of shifts in the social status and economic position
of the dreamer. Foucault's point is that in his oneirology
Artemidorus, in this a typical Ancient, regarded sexuality as
eminently 'relational', i.e., deeply linked to social relations.
Augustine, on the other hand, minimized relationship to others,
concentrating instead on the problem of the self in the conflict of will
versus sex. In the famous fourteenth book of *The City of God*, he
opposed pre-lapsarian sex to intercourse after the Fall. Sex in our
sinful state is to Augustine the epitome of loss of self-control. Giving
a dramatic twist to the old idea of the coitus as a small epilepsy
(above, page 128), Augustine wrote that the sexual act is a ghastly
spasm, the body shaken by appalling jerks. Sex in paradise, by
contrast, was a marvel of self-mastery. Adam's whole body made sex,
just as our fingers can control each of their gestures; sex and will were
not yet dissociated. The lesson is clear: since early Christian thought,
eros was put under the starkest suspicion. Confessional man replaced
the aesthetics of pleasure by a painful, censorious, repressive
introspection of debased desire. Spiritual overcoming of the libido
ceased to consist, as in Plato, in looking upwards and remembering
what the soul knew long ago but had forgotten; rather, it came to
consist in a constant watch-out for sin, in looking 'continuously
downwards or inwards in order to decipher, among the movements of
the soul, which ones come from the libido'.[22]

Experts on ancient thought will no doubt quickly assess Foucault's
interpretations and conclusions. One thing is sure: he now discusses
scholars' opinions far more often than in all his other historical vistas

put together. Moreover, the quality of the literature consulted is also higher, and the literature itself generally up-to-date; for someone who, in *The Will to Truth*, was still relying on such flimsy historiographic support as Steven Marcus's *The Other Victorians* (1966), the progress has been far from negligible. And although it is incomparably less easy to dust off a completely forgotten ancient text in Greek or Latin than to unearth abstruse treaties of the Renaissance or obscure disciplinary codes of 1800, so that in his archaeology of sexuality Foucault's scholarship was bound to show in more conventional, less spectacular ways, in the end it was here rather than in his prior labours that he stood closer to the conquering spirit of new historiography - a path breaking mood pioneered by maverick historians such as Philippe Ariès, the chronicler of changing attitudes towards childhood and death, on whose own death Foucault wrote in a hero-worshipping vein for *Le Nouvel Observateur* (inelegantly bashing Lawrence Stone in the process); and a spirit which Pierre Nora and a distinguished team of fellow historians tried to theorize, mapping out 'new problems, new approaches and new objects' for history, in the three-volume survey, *Faire de l'histoire* (1977).

True, one could quibble over the stand of some interpretations in view of recent research. For instance, Foucault's picture of pederasty sounds a little bit undeveloped from a sociological viewpoint. He is of course pretty realistic about the ancient practice; not for a moment does he mistake Xenophon's Socratic over-spiritualization of homosexual *eros* for the social truth. Yet in the end his analysis turns out to be less sociologically illuminating than that of K.J. Dover, despite his several references to Dover's *Greek Homosexuality* (1978). Now Dover commands the field in the reinterpretation of Greek pederasty, thanks to his resolute demolition of the 'Doric' thesis, a German construct based on the assumption that the roots of *l'amour grec* are to be found in martial comradeship (a brilliant representative of the Doric theory, E. Bethe, writing shortly before the First World War, explained that Hellenic pederasty rested on a spermatic concept of the soul: man's best virtues being located in his sperm, sodomy was believed to be the best way to communicate bravery to a young warrior...). Dover rejected all this 'Prussian' militaristic tosh and stressed that, in the *polis*, everything encouraged conspicuous male sociability. Foucault, as we saw, was alive to the different status of wives and ephebes, but he did not dwell on the mechanics of their social setting and their respective situational logics. However, as far as I can see, nothing that he says seems to be in contradiction with the best available scholarship on the subject.

These two volumes also seem to contain some significant shifts in Foucault's historiography. Some of the changes simply reinforce trends already discernible in *The Will to Truth* if not before, such as the attenuation of caesuralism (the break with break theory) and the frank admission of evolutionary phenomena. He speaks of a 'very slow evolution' from paganism into Christianity, and again, from classical ancient erotics to the *ars amandi* of late Antiquity.[23] Other shifts, however, bring new factors into play, including the religious subject matter. In 1970, interviewing Foucault with S.P. Rouanet at his new home at Rue Vaugirard, I asked Foucault whether he intended to extend 'archaeological' history to the religious experience. He answered that he did, but added that his real interest in this field was witchcraft.[24] Yet his last, still unpublished book - *Les Aveux de la chair* (Confessions of the Flesh) the fourth and final volume of *The History of Sexuality* - is a reflection on Christianity as the quintessence of 'confessional' faith.

Like his master Nietzsche, Foucault clearly dislikes the Christian cast of mind. However, nothing in the preceding volumes, where Christianity is often alluded to as the negative, as it were, of ancient erotics, matches the Manichaean dramatization of history which he used to indulge in before. To be sure, in Foucaldian Christianity, self-technology and control, in the ugly sense of repressive domination, tend to merge. But there seems to be less insistence on casting cultural forms or ages into the role of the villain. The long shadow of the Christian hermeneutics of self and sin draws less reproach from Foucault than the Big Confinement, the psychiatrization of madness, epistemic anthropologism or the modern prison system. Had the *Kulturkritiker* mellowed, or was there something in his new subject to explain it?

I suspect the truth is in the latter hypothesis - and in what constitutes a paradox in the history of Foucaldian thought. Let me explain why. In his first original flight, *Madness and Civilization*, Foucault was faced with the problem of what insanity meant to others - the sane, judges of madmen. At the other extreme of his rich historico-philosophical journey, he came to grips with the problem of what sex mean *to oneself* - the meaning of the libido as the most explosive material to be shaped by active selfhood. But here an intriguing point suggests itself: if Foucault's last theme was, through sexuality, self-assertion or self-mastery or then sin-ridden introspection, *what of his long-standing subject-phobia?* Both *enkrateia* and confession presuppose a full-grown subjectivity - the very thing Foucault (in this a good structuralist almost to the last) taught us to despise as a metaphysical mirage and to discard as an analytical tool in the explanation of social processes. True, we saw him stress the focus on the subject in his later work. But the issue we are now raising is an entirely distinct proposition: it does not concern subjectivity as a dependent variable (historical product of power) but the subject as an independent variable - as a force shaping conduct. Did he come to focus on the subject not just as a theme but also as a genuine factor?

Let me rephrase it: could it be that, in Foucault's work in the 1980s, the subject - and, together with it, plain human agency - was eventually, if tacitly, vindicated, or re-entered the scene by stealth? Was Foucault secretly making his peace with the subject? I for one find it hard to square the historical tale of *The History of Sexuality* with the power/knowledge *Leitmotiv*, where the subject is but an instrument of domination. For, if the Christian 'confessing animal' can still be construed as something of the kind, since he is ever watching his desire under the compulsion of a moral Law, the encratic subject of pagan Antiquity certainly cannot. Here we reach a clear-cut case of healthy subject, conspicuously unrelated to social domination over the individual. To some other theorists, also probing the deep meanings of cultural history, there would be nothing odd in equating the progress of the West with a widespread growth in self-control. Norbert Elias in *The Civilising Process* (1939) argued that civilization amounts above all to a general shift from social constraints to self-constraint (*Selbstzwang*). The trouble with Foucault is that, in his stark rejection of positive values pertaining to 'civilization' as an early modern process enhanced by the Enlightenment and then by Victorian liberalism, he could not in good logic countenance such an assessment of historical outcomes. Yet from *L'Usage des plaisirs* onwards, he set great store by the strength of will of the subject.

'Will' is a key concept here. Indeed, much of what Foucault says on *enkrateia* and the concern for self of the determinate Stoic could be read in the light of modern studies on the history of the idea of will in legal and philosophical thought. It would have been very instructive to have Foucault comment on a recent work such as *The Theory of Will in Classical Antiquity* (1982) by the Heidelberg classicist, Albrecht Dihle. To Professor Dihle, the concept of the will as a faculty of mind independent from intellect or emotion was never employed in ancient Greek theory - it was essentially a creation of St Augustine, who first used will (*voluntas*) in the modern Western sense, to refer to the very core of moral man. Foucault devoted *Les Aveux de la chair* - the only historical part of *The History of Sexuality* dwelling on Christianity - to the palaeo-Christian theology of the so-called Fathers of the Church, among whom Augustine was such a towering figure. What is more, as Dihle makes clear, the crucial role attributed to will in St Augustine's interlocked systems of psychology and theology resulted mainly from intensive self-examination, as witnessed by his *Confessions*,[25] and intensive self-examination is exactly what Foucault takes as the defining trait of 'confessional man' - the moral style of Christianity, later secularized in modern man, as regards the technology of the self.

Now the Augustinian will concept, based as it was on introspection and destined to such centrality in Christian doctrine, did not evolve out of a moral-sexual but a moral-religious problematic. Moreover, if, as Foucault rightly claims, self-mastery and soul-building (Cicero's *cultura animi*) were so prominent in pagan Antiquity, how come the Greeks and Romans never developed a concept of will? Contrariwise, one might retort that it was only when sin and salvation came to dominate the concerns of pre-modern thought that the autonomous will - the chief structure of the subject - emerged in the mind of the West, never to dwindle since, not even after the ebbing of faith as a great shaper of Western culture. In which case, Foucault's analysis did not fall too wide of the mark. At all events, as Raymond Bellour was quick to notice, now that so many sex taboos are gone, the pressing question which remains with us is: how is each one of us to (re)define himself or herself as a subject?[26] In our hedonic culture, it is indeed probable that such redefinition takes place first and foremost in relation to pleasure and desire. If so, Foucault's genealogy of the 'man of desire' is not without relevance to his otherwise sorry project of a critical history of the present.

10. Portrait of the neo-anarchist

What is the core meaning of the work of Michel Foucault, archaeologist of thought, genealogist of power/knowledge, 'historian of the present'? Book-length answers to this question abound. Eleven years ago, closing her *Foucault et l'archéologie du savoir*, Angèle Kremer-Marietti wondered whether there was a original metaphor underpinning his whole enterprise. She found it in the *anatomic gaze*. Just as the anatomist dissects corpses working from the surface into depth, laying bare all the details of the bodily layers, fibre by fibre, tissue by tissue, membrane by membrane, sinew by sinew, without ever being able to grasp the secret of life, so the 'archaeological' historian dissects many discourses and practices, denying himself the mirage of that global understanding of bygone cultural totalities once pursued by neo-idealist philosopher-historians. Such is the distance from Dilthey to Foucault. A doctor's son, the archaeologist of discourse brought history under the scalpel. So much, then, for the character of his endeavour. What about the nature of its outcome? Here the answers widely diverge. To Pamela Major-Poetzl (*Michel Foucault's Archaeology of Western Culture*, 1983), the gist of Foucault's most valuable contribution is a new paradigm for the human sciences based on principles analogous to field theory in modern physics. Sticking to 'archaeology', Major-Poetzl claims that it is, like modern physics, an abstract model imposing order on an experience of disorder. Her view is therefore poles apart from Hubert Dreyfus and Paul Rabinow's in *Michel Foucault: Beyond Structuralism and Hermeneutics* (1982). To Dreyfus and Rabinow, Foucault's wisdom was his move away from archaeology and its parastructuralist assumptions towards an 'interpretative analytics' of 'power, truth and the body'; in a nutshell, the best Foucault is his genealogy rather than his archaeology; or, if you wish, its post-structuralism rather than its quasi-structuralism. Yet if one bears in mind the Nietzschean temper of Foucaldian thought (admittedly more pronounced after *Les Mots et les choses*) one soon realizes that the gap between Foucault the archaeologist and Foucault the genealogist is no chasm. The centrality of Nietzsche in Foucault's outlook is emphasised by his main translator, Alan Sheridan, in *Michel Foucault: the Will to Truth* (1980). Sheridan suggests that his hero is the Nietzsche of our own *fin de siècle*. A provocative prospect, far more interesting than those who - like Annie Guédez in her much earlier *Foucault* (1972), ended up by practically annexing archaeology, on the grounds of its antipositivism, to the lyrically humanist social theory of Gurvitch and Henri Lefebvre[1] - two notorious opponents of structuralism because of the latter's alleged objectivism and 'technocratism'. One of the rather few good things in the garrulous study by Charles Lemert and Garth Gillan, *Michel Foucault: Social Theory and Transgression* (1982), is the pinpointing of a Nietzschean streak in Foucault via Bataille.[2]

However, acknowledging the 'Nietzsche connection' does not prevent further controversy about Foucault's ultimate position in radical theory. While Barry Smart (*Foucault, Marxism and Critique*, 1983) thinks Foucaldian 'transgressive thought' is an asset in that it frees critique of the fallacies involved in the Marxist ideal of a 'higher rationality' both in knowledge (as a 'science of history') and in actual history (as socialism, now as discredited as capitalism),[3] Colin Gordon takes the opposite view. He, too, sees the need for new 'logics of revolt'; but he does not pit Foucault's identification of power apparatuses against Marxist theory.[4] To Sheridan, Foucault's political anatomy, a 'radical break' with both left and right, constitutes a new political theory and practice emerging from the discredit of Marxism.[5] To Smart, it indeed emerges from Marxism's disrepute, but is no new political theory and practice, just a very useful 'critique'. To Gordon, Foucault identifies forms of power hitherto neglected - but there is no need to describe his enterprise as a Nietzschean challenge to Marxism.

How are we to choose between these readings? First of all, as far as I can see, there is no way of minimizing the Nietzsche connection in

Foucault's work. The latter is arguably the prime instance of neo-Nietzscheanism in contemporary Western thought – and no doubt a highly original use of Nietzsche to boot. There is a well-known characterization of French philosophy since the war, originally proposed by Vincent Descombes, to the effect that while in the 1940s the dominant influence on French thought were the three Hs – Hegel, Husserl, Heidegger – the prevailing matrix in the 1960s shifted towards the three 'masters of suspicion': Marx, Nietzsche, Freud. Now this is especially true of Foucault, over whose historico-philosophical frescoes there hovers the shadow of Nietzschean irrationalism unstained by any major echo from Hegel, Husserl or Heidegger. In chapter VII of *The Joyous Science* Nietzsche gives a list of histories yet to be written: the history of love, greed, envy, conscience, pity and cruelty; a comparative history of law; another of penalties. ... Can anyone read this without instantly recognizing at least a part of Foucault's historical enterprise?

Once we agree on the strategic meaning of his Nietzschean roots, all that remains to be done is to ascertain the *value* of Foucault's creative reprise of Nietzsche. In what I personally reckon the most thoughtful book as yet written on Foucault – *Linguaggio, potere, individuo* (1979) – Vittorio Cotesta sums up his assessment of him by saying yes to the historian and no to his metaphysics of alienation. Cotesta praises Foucault's historical inquiries, but cannot bring himself to accept his political anthropology, because it is devoid of any vision of non-alienated social relations.[6] Like Nietzsche, Foucault holds the individual's will to power as a datum which is also an unavoidable fatum. The forms of such *libido dominandi* always change throughout history: its nature, never. Insofar as will to power is a synonym of man, there can be no social overcoming of alienation imposed by violence. The struggle goes on and on. Foucault does not combat existing powers for the sake of a nobler, more humane authority; he just fights them because they, too, are no more legitimate than those forces, or resistances, that oppose them. This is too bitter a pill to swallow in Italy, where oppositional culture remains largely untouched by the Parisian cynicism which followed existentialism, as a kind of ideological hangover. Accordingly,

Cotesta tries to keep Foucault's critical history cleansed of such a sombre, nasty view of man.

There are, however, two big problems with this appraisal of Foucault. First, his history – as, I daresay, has been abundantly demonstrated throughout this book – is far from being always sound. No doubt it often opens up new perspectives and has thereby heuristic virtues. But its conceptual muddles and explanatory weaknesses (and mark: it is always an argumentative history, an *histoire à thèse*) more than outweigh its real contributions. Foucault's historical evidence is too selective and distorted, his interpretations too sweeping and too biased. Thus in the end, far from counting by itself, as research or insight, his history stands or falls with his *Weltanschauung* – and therefore falls.

To be sure, over and again Foucault kept denying that he was writing normal history. The last time (I think) was in the introduction to *L'Usage des plaisirs*, where he once more warned that his studies were 'of history', not of 'a historian'. However, no amount of equivocation can get him off the hook on this point. Historian or not, he constantly worked on the assumption that he was being faithful to each age's outlook on each relevant subject (insanity, knowledge, punishment, sex) and that his documents (e.g., medical and administrative records, old treatises of many a discipline, prison files, the literature of sexual ethics, etc.) could prove him right. The very fact that he used words like 'documents' (as he last did at the outset of *L'Usage des plaisirs*) shows that for all his 'Nietzschean' affectation of contempt for objective truth, he liked to have it speak for him as much as any conventional historian. In other words, whatever kind of historiography he was up to – the historians' one, or any other – Foucault was the first to claim that the evidence was on his side. Therefore, we can hardly exempt his historical analyses from the standard assessment of such studies. Hence our right to ask: are his interpretations borne out by the record, or are they too strained or too fanciful? Now while some of them are truly suggestive and even cast a genuinely new light on the historical evidence, many others are, as we saw, just tall orders largely unsupported by the facts. No more, no less.

Secondly, the yes-to-the-historian, no-to-the-(Nietzschean)-phil-osopher verdict tends to overlook a rather important aspect: Foucault is a Nietzschean all right, a Nietzschean in many crucial regards, but not quite a Nietzschean from top to toe. As recalled, he may even sound un-Nietzschean in his mood of elegant *Kulturpessimismus*. True, what he says on the death of man at the close of both *Les Mots et les choses* and *The Archaeology of Knowledge* is no threnody, no dirge-like lament; but neither does it seem an outburst of true *amor fati*, a tone of hope in defiance. Nietzsche was a nervous but cheerful thinker. No so Foucault. Even Ian Hacking, the Stanford philosopher who writes most sympathetically about him, grants that, by assuming that optimism and pessimism cease to make sense once you get rid of anthropologism and the humanist myth of a transcendental subject, Foucault offers us 'no surrogate for whatever it is that springs eternal in the human heart'.[7] Nietzsche, by contrast, conjured up the Overman and his joyful overcoming of nihilism, the soul of decadence. Deep down, perhaps, Foucault's thought is a half-way house between the assertive Nietzschean ethos and the modern reluctance about morale. He is enough of a Nietzschean to shun nostalgia – but he is enough of a 'modern' to display a basic scepticism on our cultural prospects.

Now as we have also seen, one of the unmistakable marks of Foucault's departure from Nietzsche's attitude towards modern history is his systematic disparagement of the Enlightenment. Lady Carlisle, the daunting Victorian lady who was the mother-in-law of Gilbert Murray, used to say: 'If anyone comes into my house who doesn't believe in progress, out he must go.'[8] In Foucault's mental abode, anyone who said a kind word on the Enlightenment risked the same treatment as Lady Carlisle's wretched non-progressivist guests – out he had to go! Nothing in Foucault makes one think he liked 'the stupid nineteenth century', as the phrase (in fact, a pearl of French reactionary ideology signed by Léon Bloy) has it; but he also dislikes what the Comteans called 'the critical age': the century of progress and critique which ended up in the two revolutions still shaping the earth, the industrial and the democratic.

Marx, Nietzsche and Freud proudly saw themselves as heirs to the

Enlightenment. Foucault certainly did not. And because he didn't, he wrote a Procrustean history where the legacy of bourgeois progress is grossly disfigured, when it is not downright denied. In so doing, Foucault proved very adept at a game typical of the most questionable 'counterculture' ideology: *the remake of the meaning of modern history so as to serve the prejudices of the ongoing – and profoundly erroneous – revolt against the Enlightenment as a main source and paradigm of modern, rational-liberal culture.* Putting the origins of modernity in the pillory considerably reinforces that *preinterpretation of the world* to which countercultural thought, from Marcuse and Laing to Illich and Foucault, is so fond of. *C'est la faute à Voltaire/c'est la faute à Rousseau.* ...

There is, nevertheless, another aspect, no less decisive, which makes Foucault truly akin to Nietzsche. It deals not with their different historical temper (pessimist against optimist, lover or hater of the Enlightenment) but with their common epistemological stance. Of the three masters of suspicion, it was precisely Nietzsche who taught us to distrust reason and truth. Now Foucault is also deeply suspicious of truth-claims; to him, every knowledge, even science, is a tool of the will to power. Epistemes are merely species of the genus power apparatus;[9] particular branches of knowledge obey strategies of domination, in fact 'invent' their objects so that man and earth can be better controlled. Reason is a technology of power; science, an instrument of domination.

On the other hand, Foucault keeps a modicum of realism to grant that rules, knowledges and techniques, whatever their origin, end up by being neutral weapons, conquerable by different social forces: thus bourgeois disciplines can be transplanted to non-bourgeois systems of control (let's forget for a moment that he counted the Gulag among the former); confession can migrate from its religious context to secular society, etc.

What is more, Foucault does not give up at least one truth-claim: that his own analytics of power is true. We noticed one aspect of this by recalling his leaning on historical documents; but he extended the same claim to the present. To be sure, as he warned (in *Power/Knowledge*), what is at stake in his work is not at all a matter of emancipating truth from power, but merely 'of detaching the power of truth from the forms of hegemony, social, economic and cultural, within which it operates at the present time'. Yet just feel the ambivalence of these words: truth is always power-ridden; however, the elegant pun ('the power of truth...') insinuates the possibility of a suspension of truth's enslavement to power. 'Detachment', however brief, unties truth from the sway of social struggle, conferring on it a genuine if precarious objectivity. This impression is strengthened by the passing Gramscian note ('hegemony'), for the gist of Gramsci's theory of hegemony is the *appropriation* of culture by a ruling class for the sake of social control, not the identification of culture as such with sheer class power.

Ultimately, then, Foucault dared not to include his own theory into what he says of the intellectuals' thought: that all is fight, nothing light, in their endeavours. The *Archaeology* confessed its theory to be 'groundless' – yet it did not say that its success was a matter of coming to blows. Now if the demonstration of the truth of his analytics of power does not depend on the blunt pragmatism of the struggle, *then at least one 'pure' truth-claim subsists.* But in this case, as Cotesta was quick to notice, there arises a contradiction between the truth criteria stated by the theory (truth is might, not light) *and the apparent claim of the theory to be itself accepted as true, regardless of such criteria.*[10]

So at bottom Foucault's enterprise seems stuck on the horns of a huge epistemological dilemma: if it tells the truth, then *all* knowledge is suspect in its pretence of objectivity; but in that case, how can the theory itself vouch for its truth? It's like the famous paradox of the Cretan liar – and Foucault seemed quite unable to get out of it (which explains why he didn't even try to face it).

It may be argued that the same impasse already plagued the thought of Nietzsche but here there are some grounds for his discharge, since at least Nietzsche's primary legacy was no historical enquiry – it was just moral critique, an essayism of revulsion against decadent man. That is why he was terribly keen on the psychology of human types, professional or national (the priest and the warrior, the German and the English, etc.), rather than in any proper sociological account of historical reality. Foucault's project as a historian of the present deprives him of such an excuse. He used genealogy to debunk the truth-claims of science, yet does not present his genealogy as an open psychological parti-pris, but as a far more 'neutral' analysis.[11]

In March 1983, Jürgen Habermas delivered a couple of lectures at the Collège de France. Published under the title *Lectures on the Discourse of Modernity*, they discuss some post-structuralist streams of thought, including the later work of Foucault. To Habermas, Foucault replaced the repression/emancipation model founded by Marx and Freud (and enshrined by the 'critical theory' of his own Frankfurt school) by the analysis of a plurality of discursive and power formations which dovetail and follow each other but which, unlike the meaning structures dealt with by critical theory, cannot be differentiated according to their validity. Moreover, Habermas points out, demystifying culture only makes sense if we preserve a standard of truth capable of telling theory from ideology, knowledge from mystification.

To Habermas, the need for keeping such a standard should prevent us from dropping the Enlightenment's ideal of a 'rational critique of existing institutions'. By denying themselves a rational theory in this sense, philosophers of the first generation of the Frankfurt school, like Max Horkheimer and T. W. Adorno, ended up by relinquishing a proper theoretical approach and collapsed critique into an ad hoc negation of contemporary society. Now the point is, this abandonment of the principle of a universal reason spells 'the end of philosophy'; and Habermas discerns three main culprits of such an inglorious outcome: old Frankfurtian critique, Heidegger's irrationalist ontology, and Foucaldian genealogy.[12]

Habermas sees himself, as well as Rawls in America, as examples of rational progressivist thought; but he does not balk at dubbing thinkers like Foucault, Deleuze and Lyotard 'neo-conservative', since they lack all theoretical justification of an alternative to the social status quo in advanced capitalism.[13]

In his televised debate with Chomsky (Amsterdam, 1971), Foucault refused to draw a model society on the grounds that the task of the revolutionary is to conquer power, not to bring about justice, and that at any rate abstract notions such as truth, justice and human nature (all upheld by Chomsky) are bound to mirror the dominant class interests of our culture.[14] Habermas's criticism pinpoints the theoretical (as opposed to the ethical) plane of the same gap: the purposeful absence, in Foucault, of universalist principles, which he deems to be in league with 'humanist myths' and ultimately with the power structure of modern society.

Foucault was quite conscious of his renunciation of the universalist point of view upheld by Habermas. In its stead, he put forward the ideal of the 'specific intellectual' who would provide critical knowledge without posing as a 'master of truth and justice'. While Habermas saw universalism as a rational guarantee of truth, he could only see it as a mask of dogmatism. Universal truth was just another name for power disguised as the criterion of all knowledge. As to the Frankfurt school, Foucault acknowledged their merit in identifying as a problem the 'power effects' linked to a rationality historically defined in the West since early modern times – but he rejected the philosophical framework of their 'critical theory' because it seemed to him riveted on a metaphysics of the subject and fraught with Marxist humanism.[15]

In one of his last courses at the Collège de France Foucault discussed Kant's essay on the Enlightenment. Kant's issue, said he, was the problematic of the present (*la problématique d'une actualité*); Kant's originality in '*Was ist Aufklaerung?*' lies in the perspicuity of his outlining 'the question of the present', since the Enlightenment was then the very living moment of Western culture. Foucault stressed that philosophy ceased thereby to inquire into its own belonging to a long tradition of argument and speculation in order to see itself, for the first time, as an activity deeply involved in the fate of the community. Kant removed the question of modernity from its 'longitudinal relation with the Ancients' (so conspicuous in early modern 'battles of ancients and moderns'), and inaugurated a 'sagittal relationship' between thought and its own historical place.

In conclusion, Foucault said that far more important than preserving the remains of the Enlightenment is the task of keeping alive to its historical meaning. In other words, even when discussing the *locus classicus* of praise for the Enlightenment he found a way to snipe at its intellectual heritage. The course's last two paragraphs are still odder. They say that Kant 'founded the two great traditions shared by modern philosophy': the tradition of 'analysis of truth', namely, of constant inquiry into the conditions of true knowledge, and the tradition – launched in 'What is the Enlightenment?' – of an 'ontology of the present'. Such is, ends up Foucault, 'the philosophical choice confronted by us nowadays', *either* an analytic of truth *or* 'a critical thought taking the form of an ontology of ourselves, an ontology of the present'. The latter was the path taken by Hegel, by Nietzsche and Weber, by the Frankfurt school and by himself, Foucault.[16]

Now this very interesting statement calls for some remarks. First, its attempt to play Kant against Kant, so to speak, is highly questionable – and so is the reduction of the Frankfurt school labours to an ontology of the present (in Habermas the 'analytic of truth' is at least as important). Above all, the course sells us, not a wrong option (since there is of course nothing wrong with inquiring upon the nature of the present), but a wrong alternative. Why indeed should we think of the question of the present as something to be conducted *instead of* and ultimately, as it were, *against* the question of valid knowledge (in short: the theory of science)? Foucault seems to reason as though his sharp divide between those two pursuits were a matter of course whose legitimacy we must take for granted. In fact, however, it is nothing of the kind. For, far from being something external to the nature of the present, scientific knowledge simply inheres in modernity as its most powerful driving force. We live in a world shaped by science. Actually, as Ernest Gellner put it, while once upon a time there was science within the world, now it is as if the world were within science; science became the container, the world the content.

Consequently, no history of the present can ever be truly cogent that makes little or no room for an account of science, its nature and its impact. Nothing being more intrinsically modern than sustained cognitive growth, no critical theory of the present can succeed without a serious discussion – epistemological as well as sociological

– of science. By the same token, Foucault's decision to scrutinize 'informal knowledge' instead of looking into hard science was bound to cripple his programme. No exorcism of the transcendental subject, no detection of power mechanisms could possibly offset the loss of historical vision caused by the lack of a proper attention to world-shaping knowledge.

Piaget epitomized his strictures against Foucault by calling his work a 'structuralism without structures'. One could also deplore his cartography of epistemes without epistemology, i.e., without a theory of science. *In the end – and despite all his rhetoric of antihumanism – the 'humanist' in Foucault carried the day; and because it did, his steps towards a history of the present turned out to be more of a revulsion against modernity than a genuine, objective apprehension of its character.* For all their frequent topicality, Foucaldian genealogies have an air of exotica about them. The reason is that they never address the central concerns of our age: science, economics, nationalism and democracy. What 'ontology of the present' can do without them?

Science is, among other things, thought sitting in judgement of thought: in scientific language no one can speak as they please, but only according to universal principles of evidence and logic. Such validity of thought was no concern of Foucault. Archaeo-genealogy only knows that one cannot speak at any age of any subject: 'On ne peut pas parler à n'importe quelle époque de n'importe quoi.' (*Archaeology*, II, 3).

In his subtle comment on *The Archaeology of Knowledge*[17] Frank Kermode said that Foucault offered a negative version of those 'tacit' cognitive skills theorized by Michael Polanyi in *Personal Knowledge* (1958). Polanyi argued that intimacy with a cognitive system endows scientists with a knowledge-producing ability that cannot be specified in explicit impersonal rules. Foucault stresses the negative side of it: he contends that it is normally impossible to get out of such a tacit system of knowledge. We have been shifted from the open orbit of tacit personal knowledge into the rigid framework of what Collingwood called the 'absolute presuppositions' of a cultural age.

Now this raises a big problem for 'archaeological' history. For, as

David Leary most perceptively remarked, 'if one denies any kind of continuity in history – and it is Foucault's avowed task to demonstrate the radical discontinuity in history – then how is one to explain the possibility of doing history?'[18] How, unless we reintroduce some degree of historical continuity, can we even begin to understand the past? No White-and-Veyne hymn to the need for 'defamiliarizing history' can ever quash such a query.

But this is not all. Within the epochal grid of cognitive assumptions, the uncanny Foucaldian 'archive' of discourses 'picks up' a given 'regime of objects'. The 'what' of discourse does not antedate the emergence of discourse; rather, it is constituted by the complex set of relations obtaining between, in Foucault's own enumeration, institutions, socio-economic processes, techniques and modes of behaviour, systems of classification and characterization, etc. In short: between all relations generated by the manifold interplay of mind, nature and society. Thus the rules of discursive formation allow or forbid the what of knowledge; and the genealogist's eye seeks to pierce through the thickness of discourse to identify its historical roots – the 'why' of that 'what'. Yet neither archaeological scanning nor genealogical probing cares about the 'how' of discourse, as far as its cognitive worth is concerned. Therefore none of the two Foucaldian approaches to the world of knowledge is bent on gauging how much *real* knowledge of the world there is in it all. *The focus on power/knowledge ends up by giving short shrift to the power of knowledge*, on the cognitive as well as on the historical plane. Now the trouble is, while of course no one has a right to demand that Foucault be an epistemologist, one can very well wonder whether, as a self-appointed historian of the present, he could leave aside the 'analytics of truth' involved in science and its spread all over the globe.

So, to put it bluntly, the historian of the present bungled his project. There is no gainsaying that, in the process, he forced us to think anew on sundry past forms of knowledge, or on our attitudes, both past and present, towards madness, punishment or sex. But there is a big difference between the thoughtful historian who casts new light upon the past by raising wide-ranging questions suggested by the facts, as it were, and the doctrinaire historian who more often than not strives to compress the historical record in the Procust's bed of ideological preinterpretations. Braudel belongs to the first category; Foucault to the second.

A succinct farewell to the issue of assessing the cash-value of Foucault's historical undertakings might as well repeat that at the very least, their general degree of objectivity is below the average of the best historical research of a century which has paid Clio such an opulent tribute of first-rate studies. To be sure, this is not everybody's opinion. Actually, a widespread way of looking at it is reflected in the following sentences by Dreyfus and Rabinow:

> There is obviously no simple appeal to the facts involved in evaluating Foucault's historical theses. [...] In *L'Impossible prison* a group of nineteenth-century specialists discuss *Discipline and Punish*. Their reactions vary from cautious to condescending although they succeed in demonstrating very few places where Foucault is not in control of 'the facts'. As Foucault caustically points out, most of these historians have misunderstood his argument and hence even their minor factual corrections are simply beside the point.[19]

Now *L'Impossible prison* is the book by Léonard and others we briefly mentioned above (pages 102–3). The 'very few places' where these historians caught Foucault at loggerheads with the facts are, as we saw, far from unimportant, since they include trifles like the French Revolution or the Code Napoléon. Moreover, to suggest that they systematically misunderstood Foucault's argument is blatantly untrue. Even a cursory reading of Léonard's critical comments, for instance, shows that he grasped the main theses of *Discipline and Punish* quite well. What he did not do was to accept them whole, because his historical data often did not back them up. Structuralist masters – and Foucault, alas, was no exception – have a distressing habit of evading instead of confronting critical objections; and with just a few honourable exceptions, their sympathetic interpreters seldom discuss the criticisms levelled at their heroes, or when they do, often try to tuck them away in dismissive footnotes, just as Dreyfus and Rabinow did with *L'Impossible prison*. Those inverted commas, 'the facts', tell a lot about the concern for objectivity among Foucaldians. Yet if facts are *a priori* under suspicion, why bother about their being 'few' or many, a matter of 'minor' or major corrections? How can someone so healthily liberated from positivist superstitions fall back on such vestiges of our stupid concern with factual truth?

Jacques Bouveresse, an *avis rara* among the better known French philosophers in his championing of critical standards of thought, wrote a bold, remarkable attempt – *Le Philosophe chez les autophages* – to bring home to his fellow philosophers in France that the real task of their craft is not telling people what to think but simply teaching people, by its own example, how to think.[20] The work of Foucault, however, was a brilliant, alluring instance of a philosophizing only too eager to jettison the internal stringencies of critical thought in hot pursuit of spectacular new subjects, readily interpretable in the light of ideological bias. In this, he was of course by no means alone. Disregard for real argumentative and demonstrative cogency has become gradually but steadfastly a hallmark of much of contemporary libertarian thought. And libertarianism, indeed, is the best label for Foucault's outlook as a social theorist. More precisely, he was (though he didn't use the word) a modern anarchist; no wonder of all the master-thinkers once associated with structuralism it was he who remained closest to the spirit of '68.

I can think of at least three points where Foucault did agree with the atmosphere of perfervid anarchism which inspired the students' revolt (and actually raised the black flag of anarchy in the occupied Sorbonne of May 1968). First, like most *soixante-huitards*, Foucault favoured decentralized rather than unified, let alone disciplined, revolutionary movements. Not only was he a spontaneist, someone more akin to Rosa Luxemburg than to Lenin and Trotsky, but also an unbeliever in socialist blueprints or in socialism-building in general. 'It is possible', he contended, 'that the rough outline of a future society is supplied by the recent experiences with drugs, sex, communes, other forms of consciousness and other forms of individuality. If scientific socialism emerged from the *Utopias* of the nineteenth century, it is possible that a real socialization will emerge, in the twentieth century, from *experiences*.'[21]

Secondly, just like most leaders of the rebelliousness of the sixties, Foucault had more praise for particularist combats than for class struggle in the classical economic sense. In the issue of *Esprit*, the left Christian journal, of May 1968, Foucault extolled the fight of 'women, prisoners, conscripted soldiers, hospital patients and homosexuals' as radical and revolutionary in equal terms with 'the revolutionary movement of the proletariat'.[22] Although he saw both phenomena as directed against 'the same system of power', it was not hard to see where his heart lay. As late as 1983, in a talk with the non-Communist union leader, Edmond Maire, he was musing over ways of circumventing 'frontal' modes of class struggle.[23]

Finally, and in still closer agreement with the purest anarchist tradition, Foucault was adamant in his distrust of institutions, however revolutionary they were meant to be. His debate with French Maoists on 'popular justice' printed in *Les Temps Modernes* in 1972, is exemplary in this connection. The 'Maos', who were by then supported by Sartre, wanted to establish revolutionary tribunals. Foucault objected that revolutionary justice should dispense with courts altogether, since tribunals as such are a bourgeois institution, or rather, 'bourgeois' because they are an institution.[24]

But Foucault did not just follow anarchism. Actually, what made him a *neo-anarchist* was the addition of two new aspects to the classical theory of anarchy. First, his strict anti-Utopianism. The main anarchist thinkers of the nineteenth century were also great Utopians. Though deeply suspicious of impersonal institutions, they made a point of proposing new forms of economic and social life, such as Proudhon's mutualism or Kropotkin's cooperatives. Today's neo-anarchism, by contrast, sounds thoroughly negative. It seems to possess no *pars construens*; its beliefs consist entirely in what it refuses, not in any positive ideals as well. Secondly, in its classical dispensation, anarchism was by no means committed to irrationalism, as it now (since at least Marcuse) seems to be. On the contrary: in its greatest theorist, Kropotkin, it even took pride in its scientific basis.

Thus Foucault features as highly representative of both the defining elements of neo-anarchism: *negativism* and *irrationalism*. Whether this change of heart in anarchy has been for better or for worse is a matter I shall leave to the reader's own judgement. Could it be that modern nihilism visited these traits upon that naïve but noble tradition of social thought? Has the ghost of Bakunin, the romantic firebrand who was in his heart a voluptuary of destruction, eventually prevailed over the sane and humane spirit of Kropotkin? ...

In my view, the main casualty of the neo-anarchist plunge into irrationalism has been the critique of power itself – the very kernel of anarchist theory. The strongest point of classical anarchism, whatever its sociological shortcomings, was its shrewd acknowledgement of the social power of power, i.e., the recognition that power relations, too, are great shapers of history, instead of being just an epiphenomenon of technological and economic factors. From the outset, anarchism distrusted the Marxian idea that power could be innocent and innocuous once shorn of its underpinnings in class structure and social exploitation.

Now the conceptual mannerisms of Foucaldian 'cratology' do not seem to have built on the realism of such insights. On the contrary: by seeing power everywhere, and by equating (in most of his work) culture with domination, Foucault, as we noticed, actually greatly reduced the explanatory force of his power concepts. Leftist radicals often praise Foucaldian analysis for its ability to spot forms and levels of power overlooked by Marxism; but the truth is, in overall terms, Foucault's obsession with power did little to enhance our objective grasp of power mechanisms, past or present. Much was claimed, too little demonstrated. By turning 'countercultural', anarchism surely became more glamorous – but its cognitive bite did not become sharper for that. And Foucault – after Marcuse – was the high priest who presided over the wedding of anarchism and the counterculture.

Structuralism as an ideological climate surrendered French thought into the hands of the 'counterculture' belief-machine. A lynchpin of the countercultural campaign is the 'critical' demolition of the Enlightenment's heritage. Michel Foucault held a key role in this intellectual strategy in that we owe him the very completion of the general onslaught against the Enlightenment. Lévi-Strauss, the founder of French structuralism and its first outstanding *Kulturkritiker*, still cherishes the ideal of science and strongly dislikes one of the counterculture's chief idols: modern art, both apocalyptic and arcane. Foucault, the Nietzschean modernist, did away with such 'positivist' residues.

Not long before May 1968, talking with Paolo Caruso, an able interviewer who listened carefully to him, Lévi-Strauss and Lacan, Foucault distinguished between two historical types of philosophy. From Hegel to Husserl, philosophy purported to achieve a global apprehension of reality. Since Sartre, however, it renounced such an ambition and turned to political action.[25] Ten years later, the Italian press still found a way to refer to Foucault as '*il nuovo Sartre*'.[26] This may sound pure journalese – yet it seems to me to harbour a good deal of truth.

Foucault did not, of course, share Sartre's ideas. In Barthes, to take another master of the 1960s, there was still a far from negligible Sartrean streak, or undercurrent. In Foucault, there is, to my mind, no major Sartrean echo – but there is a whole crypto-Sartrean ethos, well encapsulated in those words to Caruso. Roger-Pol Droit in his obituary in *Le Monde* hinted at the contrast between Sartre, the overconfident and often dogmatic-sounding *maître à penser*, and Foucault, the thinker ever doubtful as to what he would be thinking the next day. Yet despite a few abrupt changes of subject matter or philosophical perspective, Foucault's tone throughout his work was far from dubitative – indeed, it sounded pretty assertive, suggesting a common intellectual style. Ernest Gellner, in his caustic piece on Sartre (in *Spectacles and Predicaments*) spoke of 'intellectual machismo' as one of the main components of the Rive Gauche spirit. In intellectual machismo, the strength of one's argument is not propped up by logical quality – rather, it is conveyed by the unflinching self-confidence of one's tone. Impressiveness, not cogency, is the thing. So it was with Shaw; so with Sartre – and so, too, with Foucault.

Moreover, Foucault also shared with Sartre an intellectual attitude. Like Sartre, he was a clever apostle of philosophy as an *art pour l'art* of revolt. Whatever else it may have meant to him, thought was preeminently, to Foucault, rebellion without a cause. And what could have been more Sartrean than the odd combination of dark pessimism (that pessimism about man and history running from *Being and Nothingness* to the *Critique of Dialectical Reason*) with political agitation? No doubt the role of Sartre belonged, since the mid-seventies, to Foucault.

The Sartrean posture of the philosopher as a non-Utopian blesser of Radical Revolt is precisely what differentiated Foucault from his main post-structuralist rival, Jacques Derrida; for in Derrida there is no discourse on power, no rhetoric of revolt. Again, behind the negativism of Foucault – that peculiar lack of positive horizons marking him off from his master Nietzsche and, in our own time, from both other Nietzscheans, like the Dionysian 'philosophers of desire', and thinkers like Habermas – there lurks the bleak stuff of Sartre's view of man and history. 'Happiness does not exist' is a statement by Foucault,[27] but it could have been signed by Sartre.

Many have noticed the kinship between Foucault's kind of writing and the Parisian market of ideas. George Huppert discerns the secret of Foucault's success in St Germain des Prés in his ability to give 'the impression of saying something radically new while, at the same time, his "discoveries" turn out, to the young reader's satisfaction, to fit supremely well into the general movement of ideas currently in vogue'.[28] The point is rather well taken. However, a qualification is, I think, in order. Foucault may not indeed have said much that is, in substance, radically new – but he was, to some extent, renewing it to radical ears.

Let me put it more clearly. For a decade or so, since the beginning of the present slump, radical thought has been everywhere in the defensive, compelled to slough off its last Utopian skins under pressure from a growing critique of social constructionism. This was especially true in the homeland of radical thinking, France. The 'nouvelle philosophie' was just a passing fad; but the effects of its unholy alliance of Popper and Solzhenitsyn are likely to last. Curiously enough, as Mitterrand's left, in many ways no less 'deradicalized' than European social democracy, attained office,

French thought appeared plunged into a veritable purge of radicalism. Michel Tatu from *Le Monde* likes to stress that while in Britain or in Germany intellectuals' anti-Communism throve during the cold war, in France those were the days of maximum flirting with the myth of revolution and socialism-building. Now we witness the ebb-tide. Yet radical rhetoric is almost a frame of mind within the French intelligentsia; it has been an ingrained habit for too long. Therefore, it is bound to linger on, no matter on how reduced a scale, even under evil stars. The stage was set, then, for some kind of thought capable of holding the fort of the Myth of Revolt – a myth fuelled by that solemn pet amusement of French intellectuals since the days of Baudelaire and Flaubert: bourgeois-bashing. Foucault's theory of power/knowledge catered for this old need with undeniable talent and consummate aplomb, not the least because it didn't waste time on trying to rekindle any of the worn-out pieties of yesterday's radical faith. Like Sartre many years ago, Foucault had learned to distil the Elixir of Pure Negation.

In the process, unfortunately, he became a central figure in a disgraceful metamorphosis of continental philosophy – a predicament deftly described and criticized by Bouveresse.[29] It all begins with the irony of a philosophy which, having loudly proclaimed the death of man (an epistemological affair, to be sure – but with carefully orchestrated moral overtones), devotes itself to the most burning problems of humanity (insanity, sex, power and punishment...) on the grounds that philosophy as an inquiry into the old abstractions such as reality and truth, subjectivity and history has fallen into abeyance. Humility? Bouveresse doubts it. For these post-philosophical philosophers mock at the claims of all knowledge, but are little prone to extend scepticism to their own comprehensive negative views on science and society. Refusing all critical debate, they seem to labour on the illusion that the absence of method and the neglect of argumentative rigour leads automatically to a virtuous grasp of 'real problems'. They do not blush to pass as writers rather than professional thinkers, yet the 'literary' cloak barely covers a huge dogmaticism.

For instance, being, of course, radically 'critical', this new philosophy indulges in a clear *non sequitur*: it often reasons as though from the fact that the readiness to recognize a delusion or a cheat in the realm of ideas and values is in itself a healthy habit of mind we should infer that every value and every idea is but false or sham. It does not seem to realize that, as Hilary Putnam shrewdly remarked,[30] to demote rationality, in a relativist way, to a mere concoction of a given historical culture is as reductionist as the logical positivist's reduction of reason to scientific calculus. And the new *skepsis*, of which Foucault was the first master, has the 'subversive cynicism' (Bouveresse) of preaching irrationalism and intellect-debunking highly placed in core institutions of the culture it so strives to undermine: it constitutes an 'official marginality'. In its negativism it profits from this without the least moral qualm.

Leo Strauss used to say that in modern times, the more we cultivate reason, the more we cultivate nihilism. Foucault has shown that it is not at all necessary to do the former in order to get the latter. He was the founding father of our *Kathedernihilismus*.

Notes

1. The historian of the present

1. See his interview in *La Quinzaine Littéraire*, 46 (1 March 1968).
2. cf. Foucault 1970, ch. VI, 7, in fine, and Foucault 1977, pp. 30-1; he used the expression 'historian of the present' in an interview with Bernard-Henri Lévy (*Le Nouvel Observateur*, 644, March 1977; tr. in *Telos*, 32, summer 1977).
3. cf. his Foreword to the Eng. tr. (1981) of Canguilhem's *The Normal and the Pathological*, the epigraph used by C. Gordon in his Afterword to Foucault 1980, and especially Foucault's interview to *Telos*, 55 (spring 1983).
4. Foucault 1972, pp. 202-3.
5. Hayden White in Sturrock 1979, p. 83. Prior to the Sturrock volume, White had been distinctly more sympathetic to Foucault's views, as shall be seen.
6. *Telos*, 55 (spring 1983), p. 200.
7. ibid, p. 202.
8. Mandelbaum 1971, p. 6.
9. Gellner 1979, ch. 1.

2. The Great Confinement

1. Foucault 1971, pp. 3 and 6.
2. ibid, p. 164.
3. ibid, p. 269.
4. ibid, p. 274.
5. Serres 1968, p. 178.
6. cf. the review by Edgar Friedenberg in the *New York Times Book Review*, 22 August 1965.
7. Eng. tr. in Foucault 1977b.

8. See his second reply to George Steiner (the reviewer of *Madness and Civilization* in the *New York Review of Books*) in *Diacritics*, vol. 1, no. 1 (fall 1971), p. 60.

9. Megill 1979, p. 478.

10. Foucault 1972, p. 47.

11. Stone, 'Madness', in the *New York Review of Books*, 16 December 1982, p. 36.

12. Midelfort in Malament (ed.) 1980.

13. On this point, see Johnston 1972, pp. 223–9.

14. For another specialist's criticism, see Peter Gay's review in *Commentary*, 40 (October 1965).

15. Wing 1978, p. 196.

16. Major-Poetzl 1983, p. 148.

17. Foucault 1972, p. 164.

3. An archaeology of the human sciences

1. Foucault 1970, p. XXII.

2. On this point, see Dreyfus and Rabinow, 1982, p. 70, and Major-Poetzl 1983, p. 90.

3. As stressed by Stove 1982, p. 6.

4. Papineau 1979, p. 42.

5. Bachelard 1949, p. 38.

6. Canguilhem 1969, pp. 204–5.

7. cf. Bachelard 1939, ch. VI ('L'Epistémologie non-cartésienne').

8. cf. Sorel, *De l'utilité du pragmatisme* (1921); excerpts in Stanley (ed.) 1976, ch. 8.

9. cf. Hyppolite 1954.

10. See on this point the judicious remarks of Paola Zambelli in the introduction to Koyré 1967, p. 37ff.

11. Koyré 1966, pp. 284–96.

4. From the prose of the world to the death of man

1. 'Die Zeit des Weltbildes' (1938), printed as the second essay of his book *Holzwege* (1950); English tr. in Heidegger 1977.

2. Dilthey 1905, ch. 1.

3. Foucault 1970, p. 55.

4. This point had also been stressed by Heidegger (see note 10 below).
5. On Velásquez' stylistic evolution, see the study of the noted expert E. Lafuente Ferrari 1960, especially pp. 89–91 and 102–13.
6. According to Velásquez' eighteenth-century biographer Antonio Palomino, quoted in John Rupert Martin 1977, p. 167.
7. These speculations have been suggested by J. R. Martin, op. cit., p. 124.
8. On all this historical background, see Lassaigne 1952, pp. 60–5.
9. Foucault 1970, p. 16.
10. ibid, p. 239.
11. ibid, p. 157.
12. ibid, p. 219.
13. ibid, p. 207.
14. ibid, p. 308.
15. ibid, p. 387 (the last paragraph in the book).
16. For these phrases (and others similar) see Foucault 1970, ch. IX, 2.
17. For all this paragraph, see Foucault 1970, ch. IX, 4.
18. Foucault 1970, ch. X, 2.
19. ibid, ch. X, 3.
20. ibid, p. 364.
21. ibid, ch. X, 5.
22. Serres 1968, pp. 193 and 198.

5. The 'archaeology' appraised

1. There remains only to say a word about something almost between the lines in the book: Foucault's remarks on the status of literature through the sequence of his epistemes. Actually, he has two ways of presenting literature in 'archaeological' terms. On the one hand, literature fills up the interstices between epistemes: thus, just as *Don Quixote* signalled the death of Renaissance knowledge, in Sade the violence of desire marked the end of the classical episteme. On the other hand, the archaeology of knowledge gave literature 'a new way of being'. Mallarmé,

assigning to poetry a reflection on language, converting literature to formalism, brought no break with the modern episteme. Rather, he led to its consummation a 'return of language' inscribed in the very nature of the fate Western culture embraced since the dawn of the nineteenth century. To Foucault, Mallarmé parallelled Nietzsche in cogently underlining the urgent issue of language. After his bethrothal of literature to intransitive language, literary art could only carve its main moments out of a heightened experience of existential limits, as in Kafka or Artaud. Foucault's idea – and ideal – of modern literature begins with Blanchot (literature as an intransitive materiality of language) and ends up with Bataille (literature as the aesthetics of transgression). No far cry from the ideology of literary structuralism. Besides, Foucault has himself been an occasional literary critic, as witnessed by his short book on the minor experimental novelist, Raymond Roussel (1963), his brilliant essay on Klossowski's *Bain de Diane* (in *Nouvelle Revue Française*, 135, March 1964) and his perceptive essay on Flaubert ('Fantasia of the Library', 1967, in Foucault 1977b, pp. 87–109). The last is very illuminating on the relations between imagination and what structuralist literary criticism calls intertextuality. He has also written on Bataille (see 'A Preface to Transgression' (1963) in Foucault 1977b) and on Blanchot (cf. his essay 'La pensée du dehors' in *Critique*, 229, June 1966).

2. cf. Foucault, 'Réponse au cercle d'épistémologie', *Cahiers pour l'analyse*, 9 (summer 1968).

3. Foucault 1970, ch. VIII, 2.

4. See G. S. Rousseau 1972, p. 241. Rousseau claims support from Yates 1964.

5. Huppert 1974, pp. 204–6.

6. On all this, see Koyré 1961, pp. 61–9, and Yates, op. cit., pp. 153, 155 and 440–3.

7. cf. Westfall 1980, p. 407.

8. On the history of this theoretical background, cf. Mittelstrass 1979, especially pp. 43–53. Kepler's own words (in his *Epitome Astronomiae Copernicanae*) are: '... et contemplari genuinam

formam aedifici mundani.' The downfall of Aristotelian physics is briefly well told in Butterfield 1957, especially ch. 4.

9. cf. Schumpeter 1954, p. 826.
10. Piaget 1970, ch. VII, 21.
11. Canguilhem 1967, pp. 612–13.
12. Foucault 1970, p. 168; emphasis added.
13. ibid, p. 217.
14. Foucault 1972, p. 16.
15. Huppert 1974, pp. 200–1.
16. Foucault 1970, p. 22.
17. Huppert, op. cit., pp. 201–3.
18. G. S. Rousseau 1972, pp. 248–9.
19. ibid., pp. 245–6. G. S. Rousseau enlists the support of two Sanctius scholars, the American R. Lakoff, a student of Chomsky – cf. his essay in *Language*, 45 (1969; pp. 343–64) – and the Englishman Richard Ogle, from the University of Essex Language Centre. Jean-Claude Chevalier's *Histoire de la Syntaxe* (1968) had already pointed out the Port-Royal debt to Sanctius.
20. See the essay by Jean-Claude Chevalier on the Port-Royal grammar in *Langages*, 7 (September 1967).
21. Miel 1973, pp. 239–40.
22. For all these historical data, see Butterfield 1957, ch. 11.
23. On this point, see Singer 1962, p. 281.
24. Burgelin 1967, p. 855.
25. Kristeller 1961, especially pp. 10, 22 and 94–103.
26. Burgelin, op. cit., p. 856.
27. Another conceptual riddle – from the viewpoint of Foucault's categories – has been pointed out by an expert on biological classification, Vernon Pratt. Pratt is overall quite complimentary to Foucault, but he notes (pp. 167–78) that in emphasizing the Cartesian character of classical natural history, reflected in the taxonomy of the age, Foucault overlooks an important un-Cartesian aspect of classical naturalists: concentrating as they did on the *external form* of organisms, the classical taxonomists were turning their backs on the Cartesian stress on *underlying* structure.

28. Gusdorf 1973, pp. 308–28.

29. cf. Chevalier, op. cit., p. 32.

30. Miel, op. cit., p. 244.

31. Hazard 1935.

32. Wade 1977, vol. I, pp. 84–6.

33. Cassirer 1932, ch. 1.

34. 'Modern paganism' is a central concept in Peter Gay's commanding study of the Enlightenment. See Gay 1966, vol. I and, on Hume, especially ch. VII, 3.

35. Foucault 1970, p. xxii.

36. White 1973, pp. 50–2. Now a chapter in White 1978.

37. White 1973, p 53.

38. Veyne, 'Foucault révolutionne l'histoire', an appendix to Veyne 1978, especially pp. 226–31 and 240.

39. Foucault 1977b, p. 142.

40. See Bellour 1971, pp. 189–207; an interview originally published in *Les Lettres Françaises*, 1187 (15 June 1967).

41. Foucault 1967, pp. 192 and 187.

6. The ironic archive

1. Foucault 1972, p. 49.

2. ibid, p. 114.

3. ibid, p. 27.

4. ibid, pp. 31 and 27.

5. ibid, p. 111.

6. cf. his interview with R. Bellour, quoted in note 97.

7. Lecourt 1972.

8. Foucault 1972, pp. 138–40.

9. Panofsky 1955, introduction (first published in T. M. Greene, ed., *The Meaning of the Humanities*, Princeton, 1940).

10. For Panofsky's critique of Wölfflin, see his essay 'Das Problem des Stils in der bildenden Kunst', *Zeitschrift für Aesthetik und allgemeine Kunstwissenschaft*, X (1915), pp. 460ff., reprinted in Panofsky 1964; there is an Italian translation by Enrico Filippini in the volume *La Prospettiva come 'forma simbolica'*, Milan: Feltrinelli, 1966 (1st ed., 1961), pp. 141–51. 'Das Problem des

Stils' comments on a lecture given by Wölfflin in Berlin in 1911 which contains in a nutshell the main thesis of Wölfflin's epoch-making *Principles of Art History* (1915).

11. Panofsky 1955, intro.; the same idea, minus the reference to Peirce, was already expressed in 'Zum Problem der Beschreibung und Inhaltsdeutung von werken der bildenden Kunst', published in the neo-Kantian journal *Logos*, XXI (1932); this essay is also reprinted in Panofsky 1964 and also translated in Italian in *La Prospettiva*, op. cit. 'Content' is also employed to name the deepest stratum of meaning in the visual arts in the introduction to Panofsky's *Studies in Iconology* (1939).

12. In this sense, the gap, correctly noticed by Podro (1982, p. 205), between Panofsky's focus on ideological content and Aby Warburg's concern with interpreting art in a context of social behaviour is a family quarrel – both are anti-formalist, 'cultural' approaches to the study of art. Art as symbol (Panofsky) or art as ritual (Warburg) are perspectives closer to each other than either is to art as pure form.

13. cf. John Dunn, 'The Identity of the History of Ideas' (1968), now in P. Laslett, W. G. Runciman and Q. Skinner (eds.) 1972; and Quentin Skinner, 'Meaning and Understanding in the History of Ideas', *History and Theory*, 8. 1(1969), pp. 3–53.

14. For all the negative definitions of the 'statement', see Foucault 1972, pp. 79–87.

15. Foucault 1972, pp. 153–4.

16. ibid, p. 129.

17. ibid, pp. 128–31.

18. cf. Foucault, 'Réponse au cercle d'épistémologie' (see note 2, ch. 5).

19. 'What is an Author?' was first published in the *Bulletin de la Société Française de Philosophie*, 63 (1969), pp. 73–104; English tr. in Foucault 1977b, pp. 113–38.

20. Foucault 1972, III, 2.

21. ibid, p. 183.

22. ibid, p. 205.

23. Megill 1979, p. 487.

24. Deleuze 1972, pp. 44–5 (my translation).
25. Foucault 1972, p. 216 (the English text of *L'Ordre du discours* follows the main text in the American edition of *The Archaeology of Knowledge*).
26. Foucault 1972, p. 229.

7. Charting carceral society

1. 'The Intellectuals and Power', originally in *L'Arc*, 49 (March 1972), pp. 3–10; tr. in *Telos*, 16 (summer 1973), reprinted in Foucault 1977b, pp. 205–17.
2. Foucault 1977a, pp. 60–1.
3. Kantorowicz 1957, ch. 2.
4. Foucault 1977a, p. 102.
5. ibid, p. 82.
6. ibid, p. 169.
7. idem.
8. ibid, p. 199.
9. For the last three paragraphs, see Foucault 1977a, III, 1 (pp. 135–69).
10. ibid, p. 178.
11. ibid, pp. 184–94.
12. ibid, pp. 191 and 305.
13. ibid, pp. 271–2 and 277.
14. ibid, pp. 298–304.
15. ibid, p. 228.
16. ibid, p. 217.
17. For a good criticism of *Les Mots et les choses* on this account, see Pelorson 1970.
18. Foucault 1977a, p. 318.
19. ibid, pp. 216–17.
20. Léonard, in Perrot (ed.) 1980, p. 19.
21. Foucault 1977a, p. 25.
22. ibid, pp. 29–30.
23. ibid, p. 27.
24. Léonard, loc. cit., pp. 11–12.

25. Venturi 1971, pp. 103–5. Venturi mentions Hans Müller, *Ursprung und Geschichte des Wortes 'Sozialismus' und seiner Verwandten*, Hanover, 1967, on the previous Latin usage of 'socialist'.

26. Venturi, op. cit., p. 114.

27. For this criticism, see Robert Brown's review of *Discipline and Punish* in the *TLS*, 16 June 1978.

28. cf. K. Williams's entry on Foucault in Wintle (ed.) 1981.

29. Elster 1983, pp. 101–5.

30. Léonard, loc. cit., p. 14.

8. Foucault's 'cratology'

1. See Colin Gordon's afterword to Foucault 1980, p. 239.

2. Foucault 1977a, p. 194.

3. Foucault 1980, pp. 217 and 220–1.

4. For all this paragraph and its quotes, see Foucault 1980, pp. 87–90.

5. ibid, pp. 91–2.

6. cf. *La Quinzaine Littéraire*, 247 (1–15 January 1977). My translation.

7. cf. *Le Nouvel Observateur*, 12 March 1977, p. 105.

8. Foucault 1978, p. 93.

9. Foucault 1980, p. 98.

10. ibid, pp. 104–5 and 151.

11. ibid, pp. 99 and 96.

12. ibid, p. 156.

13. Gordon, in Foucault 1980, pp. 246–7 and 255.

14. Ruiz-Miguel 1983, p. 292.

15. Dews 1984, pp. 86–7.

16. Foucault 1977b, p. 208.

17. ibid, p. 222.

18. cf. *Le Nouvel Observateur*, 26 January 1976. Translated and abridged as 'The Politics of Crime' in *Partisan Review*, vol. 43, no. 3 (1976), pp. 453–9.

19. idem.
20. cf. *Le Nouvel Observateur*, 12 March 1977, pp. 113 and 124.
21. *Le Nouvel Observateur*, 9 May 1977.
22. cf. Foucault 1977b, pp. 212–16 (from 'Intellectuals and Power'). Cf. Adorno: 'When I made my theoretical model, I could not have guessed that people would want to realize it with Molotov cocktails' (*apud* Jay 1984, p. 55).
23. Interview with Jean-Louis Ézine in *Nouvelles littéraires*, 2477 (17–23 March 1975).
24. Dews, loc. cit., p. 92.
25. See the essay on Foucault in Said 1984.

9. Politics of the body, techniques of the soul

1. Foucault, *London Review of Books*, 21 May–3 June 1981, p. 5.
2. Foucault 1978, p. 58.
3. ibid, p. 59.
4. ibid, p. 24.
5. ibid, p. 60.
6. *Le Nouvel Observateur*, 12 March 1977, p. 105.
7. Foucault 1978, p. 22.
8. Gay 1984, p. 468.
9. Foucault 1980, p. 211. This dialogue from 1977, 'The confession of the flesh', ch. 11 in *Power/Knowledge*, was originally published in *Ornicar*, a journal edited by the department of psychoanalysis of the University of Vincennes.
10. Foucault 1980, pp. 196–7.
11. Foucault 1984a, pp. 10–12.
12. ibid, p. 19. My (free) translation.
13. For the last paragraphs, cf. Foucault 1984a, pp. 20–9 and 36–8. The 'elephant pattern' was already mentioned by Foucault in the *London Review of Books* article (see note 1 above), p. 5, whence comes the quote.
14. cf. Foucault 1984a, pp. 205–48.
15. ibid., pp. 267–8. My translation.
16. idem.

17. Foucault 1984b, p. 166. For the preceding remarks in the same paragraph, see especially ibid, pp. 53–5 and 143–6.
18. ibid, pp. 229–30.
19. *London Review of Books*, 21 May–3 June 1981, p. 5.
20. Foucault 1984a, p. 106.
21. Foucault 1984b, pp. 16–50.
22. Foucault, *London Review of Books*, cit., p. 5.
23. Foucault 1984a, p. 74: 1984b, p. 50.
24. cf. Rouanet (ed.) 1971, pp. 40–1.
25. Dihle 1982, p. 127.
26. Bellour, 'Une rêverie morale' (a review of *L'Usage des plaisirs* and *Le Souci de soi*), *Magazine Littéraire*, pp. 27–29.

10. Portrait of the neo-anarchist

1. Guedez 1972, pp. 104–6.
2. Lemert and Gillan 1982, pp. 22–5.
3. Smart 1983, pp. 136–7.
4. Gordon, in Foucault 1980, pp. 255–8.
5. Sheridan 1980, pp. 218 and 221.
6. Cotesta 1979, p. 172.
7. Hacking, review of *Power/Knowledge*, *New York Review of Books*, 14 May 1981, p. 37.
8. As told by J. Enoch Powell in an article on Francis West's biography of Gilbert Murray, *TLS*, 27 April 1984.
9. cf. Foucault 1980, p. 197.
10. Cotesta, op. cit., pp. 178–80.
11. Conversely, it can be argued that Nietzsche, for all his primary capacity as a moralist, not a historian or an epistemologist, does evince an attitude towards truth which, despite common ideas to the contrary, was quite compatible with an empirical-minded *cognitivism* of a fallibilist brand, and displayed in any case a strong dislike of intellectual nihilism and systematic scepticism. For a cogent claim along such lines, see Wilcox 1974, passim and especially chs. 2, 4 and 7. Wilcox's no-nonsense approach is further evidence that Nietzsche can well be worshipped in St

Germain des Prés, but eventually gets far better studied in Binghamton, NY.

12. Habermas 1985, passim.

13. cf. Rorty 1984, pp. 181–97, for a good survey of Habermas's discussion.

14. cf. Chomsky and Foucault in Elders (ed.) 1974. Chomsky comments on their disagreement in Chomsky 1979, pp. 74–80.

15. Trombadori 1981, pp. 64–5.

16. An excerpt of the course has been published by *Magazine Littéraire*, 207, May 1984; see p. 39.

17. Kermode, 'Crisis Critic', *New York Review of Books*, 17 May 1973, pp. 37–9.

18. David E. Leary, 'Michel Foucault, an Historian of the Sciences Humaines', *Journal of the History of the Behavioral Sciences*, 12 (1976), p. 293.

19. Dreyfus and Rabinow 1982, p. 126.

20. Bouveresse 1984.

21. Foucault 1977b, p. 231.

22. cf. Foucault, 'Réponse à une question', *Esprit*, 371 (May 1968), pp. 850–74. Eng. tr. as 'History, Discourse and Discontinuity' in *Salmagundi*, 20 (summer-fall 1972), pp. 225–48.

23. cf. *Le Débat*, 25 (May 1983), p. 9.

24. 'Sur la justice populaire: débat avec les maos', *Les Temps Modernes*, 310 bis (1972), pp. 335–66; now ch. 1 in Foucault 1980.

25. See his interview with Paolo Caruso (1967) in Caruso 1969.

26. cf. *L'Europeo*, 18 February 1977.

27. cf. Caruso interview (see note 25).

28. Huppert 1974, p. 191.

29. Bouveresse, op. cit., especially pp. 13–14, 44, 85–6, 107, 150, 162 and 172–4.

30. Putnam 1981, pp. 126 and 161–2.

Bibliography

I. Works by Foucault

BOOKS

FOUCAULT 1961: *Folie et déraison: historie de la folie à l'âge classique*. Paris: Plon.

FOUCAULT 1963: *Raymond Roussel*. Paris: Gallimard.

FOUCAULT 1970: *The Order of Things: an Archaeology of the Human Sciences*. New York: Random House; tr. by Alan Sheridan-Smith of *Les Mots et les choses: une archéologie des sciences humaines*. Paris: Gallimard, 1966.

FOUCAULT 1971: *Madness and Civilization: a History of Insanity in the Age of Reason*. London: Tavistock, paperback edition (1st ed., New York: Mentor Books, 1965); tr. by Richard Howard of *Histoire de la folie à l'âge classique*. Paris: Gallimard, 1964.

FOUCAULT 1972: *The Archaeology of Knowledge*. New York: Harper and Row; tr. by A. M. Sheridan-Smith of *L'Archéologie du savoir*. Paris: Gallimard, 1969. Contains in appendix a tr. by R. Swyer of *L'Ordre du discours: leçon inaugurale au Collège de France prononcée le 2 décembre 1970*. Paris: Gallimard, 1971.

FOUCAULT 1973: *The Birth of the Clinic: an Archaeology of Medical Perception*. New York: Vintage Books; tr. by A. M. Sheridan-Smith of *Naissance de la clinique: une archéologie du regard médical*. Paris: Presses Universitaires de France, 1963.

FOUCAULT 1976: *Mental Illness and Psychology*. New York: Harper Colophon Books; tr. by Alan Sheridan of *Maladie mentale et psychologie*. Paris: Presses Universitaires de France, 1962. (First edition, 1954.)

FOUCAULT 1977a: *Discipline and Punish: the Birth of the Prison.* New York: Pantheon; tr. by Alan Sheridan of *Surveiller et punir: naissance de la prison.* Paris: Gallimard, 1975.

FOUCAULT 1977b: *Language, Counter-Memory, Practice: Selected Essays and Interviews.* Ithaca: Cornell University Press. Edited, with an introduction, by Donald F. Bouchard; tr. By Donald F. Bouchard and Sherry Simon.

FOUCAULT 1978: *The History of Sexuality*, volume 1: *An Introduction.* New York: Pantheon; tr. by Robert Hurley of *Histoire de la sexualité, I: La Volonté de savoir.* Paris: Gallimard, 1976.

FOUCAULT 1980: *Power/Knowledge: Selected Interviews and Other Writings 1972–1977.* Brighton, Sussex: The Harvester Press. Edited, with a preface, by Colin Gordon, Leo Marshall, John Meplam and Kate Soper.

FOUCAULT 1984a: *Histoire de la sexualité, 2: L'Usage des plaisirs.* Paris: Gallimard.

FOUCAULT 1984b: *Histoire de la sexualité, 3: Le Souci de soi.* Paris: Gallimard.

FOUCAULT 1985: *The Foucault Reader.* New York: Pantheon. Edited by Paul Rabinow.

INTERVIEWS

CARUSO, Paolo: *Conversazioni con Claude Lévi-Strauss, Michel Foucault, Jacques Lacan.* Milan: Mursia, 1969.

TROMBADORI, Duccio: *Colloqui con Foucault.* Salerno: 10/17, 1981.

FOUCAULT, Michel *et al.*: *I, Pierre Rivière, having slaughtered my mother, my sister and my brother...: A case of parricide in the 19th century.* New York: Pantheon, 1975; tr. by Frank Jellinek of *Moi, Pierre Rivière, ayant égorgé ma mère, ma soeur et mon frère...: Un cas de parricide au XIXè siècle.* Paris: Gallimard, 1973.

II. Books on Foucault

BAUDRILLARD, Jean: *Oublier Foucault.* Paris: Édition Galilée, 1977. Tr. by Nicole Dufresne as 'Forgetting Foucault' in *Humanities in Society*, 3 (winter 1980), pp. 87–111.

COOPER, Barry: *Michel Foucault: an Introduction to his Thought.* Toronto: Edwin Mellen, 1981.

COTESTA, Vittorio: *Linguaggio, Potere, Individuo: Saggio su Michel Foucault.* Bari: Dedalo Libri, 1979.

COUSINS, Mark and HUSSAIN, Athar: *Michel Foucault.* London: Macmillan, 1984.

DELEUZE, Gilles: *Un Nouvel archiviste.* Paris: Fata Morgana, 1972.

DREYFUS, Hubert L. and RABINOW, Paul: *Michel Foucault: Beyond Structuralism and Hermeneutics.* With an Afterword by Michel Foucault. Brighton, Sussex: The Harvester Press, 1982.

GUÉDEZ, Annie: *Foucault.* Paris: Éditions Universitaires, 1972.

KREMER-MARIETTI, Angèle: *Foucault et l'archéologie du savoir.* Paris: Seghers, 1974.

LEMERT, Charles C. and GILLAN, Garth: *Michel Foucault: Social Theory and Transgression.* New York: Columbia University Press, 1982.

MAJOR-POETZL, Pamela: *Michel Foucault's Archaeology of Western Culture.* Brighton, Sussex: The Harvester Press, 1983.

PERROT, Michel (ed.): *L'Impossible prison: recherches sur le système pénitentiaire au XIXè siècle. Débat avec Michel Foucault.* Paris: Seuil, 1980.

POSTER, Mark: *Foucault, Marxism and History – mode of production versus mode of information.* Cambridge: Polity Press, 1984.

RACEVSKIS, Karlis: *Michel Foucault and the Subversion of Intellect.* Cornell University Press, 1983.

ROUANET, Sergio Paulo (ed.): *O Homem e o Discurso: a Arqueologia de Michel Foucault.* Rio de Janeiro: Tempo Brasileiro, 1971.

SHERIDAN, Alan: *Michel Foucault: the Will to Truth.* London: Tavistock Publications, 1980.

SMART, Barry: *Foucault, Marxism and Critique.* London: Routledge and Kegan Paul, 1983.

III. Books Discussing Foucault

BELLOUR, Raymond: *Le Livre des autres.* Paris: Éditions de l'Heure, 1971.

BLANCHOT, Maurice: *L'Oubli, la déraison.* In *L'entretien infini,* pp. 289–99. Paris: Gallimard, 1969.

BOUDON, Raymond and BOURRICAUD, François: *Dictionnaire Critique de la Sociologie*. Paris: Presses Universitaires de France, 1982.

CALLINICOS, Alex: *Is There a Future for Marxism?* London: Macmillan, 1982.

DERRIDA, Jacques: *Writing and Difference*, tr. by Gayatri Spivak. Chicago University Press, 1978. (French original: Paris, 1967.)

DESCOMBES, Vincent: *Modern French Philosophy*, tr. by L. Scott-Fox and J. M. Harding. Cambridge University Press, 1980. (French original: Paris, 1979.)

DUCROT, Oswald et al.: Qu'est-ce que le structuralisme? Paris: Seuil, 1928 (ch. on philosophy by François Wahl).

ELSTER, Jon: *Sour Grapes: Studies in the Subversion of Rationality*. Cambridge University Press, 1983.

KURZWEIL, Edith: *The Age of Structuralism: Lévi-Strauss to Foucault*. New York: Columbia University Press, 1980.

LECOURT, Dominique: *Marxism and Epistemology: Bachelard, Canguilhem, Foucault*, tr. by Ben Brewster. London: New Left Books, 1975. (French original: Paris, 1972.)

MALAMENT, B. C. (ed.): *After the Reformation: Essays in Honor of J. H. Hexter*, Pennsylvania, 1980.

PIAGET, Jean: *Structuralism*, tr. by Chaninah Maschler. London: Routledge and Kegan Paul, 1970. (French original: Paris, 1968.)

PUTNAM, Hilary: *Reason, Truth and History*. Cambridge University Press, 1981.

RORTY, Richard: *Consequences of Pragmatism (Essays: 1972–1980)*. Minneapolis: University of Minnesota Press, 1982.

ROSE, Gillian: *Dialectic of Nihilism*. Oxford: Blackwell, 1984 (ch. 9).

SAID, Edward W.: *Beginnings: Intention and Method*. New York: Basic Books, 1975.

—: *The World, the Text and the Critic*. London: Faber and Faber, 1984.

SEDGWICK, Peter: *Psycho Politics*. London: Pluto Press, 1982.

SERRES, Michel: *La Communication*. Paris: Les Éditions de Minuit, 1968.

SPIERENBURG, Pieter: *The Spectacle of Suffering: Execution and the*

Evolution of Repression; from a preindustrial metropolis to the European experience. Cambridge University Press, 1984.

STURROCK, John: *Structuralism and Since: from Lévi-Strauss to Derrida.* Oxford University Press, 1979.

VEYNE, Paul: *Comment on écrit l'histoire suivi de Foucault révolutionne l'histoire.* Paris: Éditions du Seuil, 1978.

WHITE, Hayden: *Tropics of Discourse.* Baltimore: Johns Hopkins University Press, 1978.

WING, J. K.: *Reasoning about Madness.* Oxford University Press, 1978.

WINTLE, Justin (ed.): *Makers of Modern Culture.* London: Routledge and Kegan Paul, 1981.

IV. Some Articles on Foucault

BARTHES, Roland: 'Savoir et folie'. *Critique*, 174 (November 1961), pp. 915–22. Tr. by Richard Howard as 'Taking Sides' in *Critical Essays*, pp. 163–170. Evanston: Northwestern University Press, 1972.

BELLOUR, Raymond: 'Une rêverie morale'. *Magazine Littéraire*, 207 (May 1984), pp. 27–30.

BERTHERAT, Yves: 'La Pensée folle'. *Esprit*, 35 (May 1967), pp. 862–81.

BOURDIEU, Pierre: 'La Mort du philosophe Michel Foucault: le plaisir de savoir'. In *Le Monde*, 27 June 1984, pp. 1 and 10.

BURGELIN, Pierre: 'L'Archéologie du savoir'. *Esprit*, 360 (May 1967), pp. 843–61.

CANGUILHEM, Georges: 'Mort de l'homme ou épuisement du cogito?' *Critique*, 242 (July 1967), pp. 599–618.

CHEVALIER, Jean-Claude: 'La Grammaire générale de Port-Royal et la critique moderne'. *Langages*, 7 (September 1977), pp. 1–33.

CRANSTON, Maurice: 'Michel Foucault'. *Encounter*, 30 (June 1968), pp. 34–42.

DEWS, Peter: 'The Nouvelle Philosophie and Foucault'. *Economy and Society*, 8, no. 2 (May 1979), pp. 127–71.

—: 'Power and Subjectivity in Foucault'. *New Left Review*, 144 (March/April 1984).

EWALD, François: 'Anatomie et corps politique'. *Critique*, 31 (December 1975), pp. 1228–65.

—: 'La Fin d'un monde'. *Magazine Littéraire*, 207 (May 1984), pp. 30–4.

FRIEDENBERG, Edgar: Review in *New York Times Book Review*, 22 August 1965.

GAUSSEN, Frédéric: 'Michel Foucault: les plaisirs et la morale'. *Le Monde*, 22 June 1984, pp. 17 and 20.

GAY, Peter: 'Chains and Couches'. *Commentary*, 40 (October 1965): pp. 93–4, 96.

GUÉDON, Jean-Claude: 'Michel Foucault: the Knowledge of Power and the Power of Knowledge'. *Bulletin of the History of Medicine*, 51 (summer 1977), pp. 245–77.

HARDING, D. W.: 'Good-by man'. *New York Review of Books*, 12 August 1971, pp. 21–2.

HUPPERT, George: 'Divinatio et Eruditio: Thoughts on Foucault'. *History and Theory*, 13 (1974), pp. 191–207.

JAMBET, Christian: 'L'Archéologie de la sexualité'. *Magazine Littéraire*, 207 (May 1984), pp. 24–7.

KERMODE, Frank: 'Crisis Critic'. *New York Review of Books*, 17 May 1973, pp. 37–9.

KREMER-MARIETTI, Angèle: 'L'Archéologie du savoir'. *Revue de Metaphysique et de Morale*, 75 (1970), pp. 355–60.

LAING, R. D.: 'The Invention of Madness'. *New Statesman*, 73 (16 June 1967), p. 843.

LASLETT, Peter: 'Under Observation'. *New Society*, 42, (1 December 1977), pp. 474–5.

LEARY, David E.: Review: 'Michel Foucault, an Historian of the Sciences Humaines'. *Journal of the History of the Behavioral Sciences*, 12 (1976), pp. 286–93.

LUCAS, Colin: 'Power and the Panopticon'. *TLS* (26 August 1975), p. 1090.

MEGILL, Allan: 'Foucault, Structuralism and the End of History'. *Journal of Modern History*, 51 (September 1979), pp. 451–503.

MIEL, Jan: 'Ideas or Epistemes: Hazard versus Foucault'. *Yale French Studies*, 49 (1973), pp. 231–45.

McDonnell, Donald J.: 'On Foucault's Philosophical Method'. *Canadian Journal of Philosophy*, 7 (September 1977), pp. 537–53.

Pelorson, Jean-Marc: 'Michel Foucault et l'Espagne'. *Pensée*, 152 (August 1970), pp. 88–99.

Peters, Michael: Extended Review. *Sociological Review*, 19 (November 1971), pp. 634–8.

Pratt, Vernon: 'Foucault and the History of Classification Theory'. *Studies in History and Philosophy of Science*, 8 (1977), pp. 163–71.

Rothman, David J.'Society and its Prisons'. *New York Times Book Review* (19 February 1978), pp. 1, 26–7.

Rousseau, G. S.: 'Whose Enlightenment? Not Man's: the Case of Michel Foucault'. *Eighteenth-Century Studies*, 6 (winter 1972–3), pp. 238–56.

Russo, François: Review. *Archives de Philosophie*, 36 (January–March 1973), pp. 64–105.

Said, Edward W.: 'The Problem of Textuality: Two Exemplary Positions'. *Critical Inquiry*, 4 (summer 1978), pp. 673–714.

Shaffer, E. S.: Review: 'The Archaeology of Michel Foucault', *Studies in History and Philosophy of Science*, 7 (1976), no. 3, pp. 269–75.

Sprinker, Michael: 'The Use and Abuse of Foucault'. *Humanities in Society*, 3 (winter 1980), pp. 1–20.

Starobinski, Jean: 'Gazing at Death'. *New York Review of Books* (22 January 1976), pp. 18, 20–2.

Steiner, George: 'The Mandarin of the Hour – Michel Foucault'. *New York Times Book Review* (28 February 1971), pp. 8, 28–31.

—: 'Steiner responds to Foucault'. *Diacritics*, 1 (winter 1971), p. 59.

Stone, Lawrence: 'Madness'. *New York Review of Books* (16 December 1983), p. 36.

Von Bülow, Katharina: 'L'Art du dire-vrai'. *Magazine Littéraire*, 207 (May 1984), p. 34–5.

Wahl, Jean: Review. *Revue de Metaphysique et de Morale*, 74, (April–June 1967), pp. 250–1.

White, Hayden: 'Foucault Decoded: Notes from Underground'. *History and Theory*, 12 (1973), pp. 23–54.

—: 'The Archaeology of Sex'. *TLS* (6 May 1977), p. 565.

WILLIAMS, Karel: 'Unproblematic Archaeology'. *Economy and Society*, 3 (February 1974), p. 41–68.

ZYSBERG, A.: 'Michel Foucault: surveiller et punir'. *Annales*, 31 (January–February 1976), pp. 168–73.

V. Miscellanea

BACHELARD, Gaston: *Le Nouvel esprit scientifique*. Paris: Presses Universitaires de France, 1934.

—: *Le Rationalisme appliqué*. Paris: Presses Universitaires de France, 1984.

BOUVERESSE, Jacques: *Le Philosophe chez les autophages*. Paris: Les Éditions de Minuit, 1984.

BUTTERFIELD, Herbert: *The Origins of Modern Science 1300–1800*. New York: The Free Press, 1957 (paperback edition, 1965).

CANGUILHEM, Georges: *Étude d'histoire et de philosophie des sciences*. Paris: Librairie Philosophique J. Vrin, 1968 (fourth edition, 1979).

CASSIRER, Ernst: *The Philosophy of the Enlightenment*. Princeton University Press, 1951. (German original: Tübingen, 1932.)

CHEVALIER, Jean-Claude: *Histoire de la syntaxe: naissance de la notion de complément dans la grammaire française (1530–1750)*. Paris: Flammarion, 1968.

DIHLE, Albrecht: *The Theory of Will in Classical Antiquity*. University of California Press, 1982.

DILTHEY, Wilhelm: *Das Erlebnis und die Dichtung*. Stuttgart: Teubner, 1905 (thirteenth edition, 1957).

DOERNER, Klaus: *Madmen and the Bourgeoisie: a Social History of Insanity and Psychiatry*. Tr. Joachim Neugroschel and Jean Steinberg. Oxford: Blackwell, 1981. (German original: 1969.)

ELDERS, Fons: *Reflexive Water: the Basic Concerns of Mankind*. London: Souvenir Press, 1974.

GAY, Peter: *The Enlightenment: an Interpretation. The Rise of Modern Paganism*. London: Wildwood House, 1966.

—: *The Bourgeois Experience: Victoria to Freud. Volume 1 – Education of the Senses*. Oxford University Press, 1984.

GELLNER, Ernest: *Spectacles and Predicaments: Essays in Social*

Theory. Cambridge University Press, 1979.

GUSDORF, Georges: *Les Sciences humaines et la conscience occidentale: VI – l'avènement des sciences humaines au siècle des lumières.* Paris: Payot, 1973.

HABERMAS, Jürgen: *Lectures on the Discourse of Modernity.* Harvard University Press, 1985.

HAZARD, Paul: *The European Mind 1680–1715.* Harmondsworth: Pelican Books, 1964; tr. by J. Lewis May of *La Crise de la conscience européene.* Paris, 1935.

HEIDEGGER, Martin: *The Question Concerning Technology and Other Essays.* Tr. by William Lovitt. New York: Harper and Row, 1977. (German original: Pfullinger 1962.)

JAY, Martin: *Adorno.* London: Fontana, 1984.

JOHNSTON, William M.: *The Austrian Mind: an Intellectual and Social History 1848–1938.* University of California Press, 1972.

KANTOROWICZ, Ernst: *The King's Two Bodies.* Princeton University Press, 1957.

KOYRÉ, Alexandre: *Études d'histoire de la pensée philosophique.* Paris: Armand Colin, 1961.

—: *Études d'histoire de la pensée scientifique.* Paris: Presses Universitaires de France, 1966.

—: *Dal mondo del pressappoco all'universo della precisione*; tr. by Paola Zambelli of part of Koyré 1961. Turin: Einaudi, 1967.

KRISTELLER, Paul Oskar: *Renaissance Thought: the Classic, Scholastic and Humanist Strains.* New York: Harper Torchbook, 1961.

LAFUENTE FERRARI, Enrique: *Velásquez.* Geneva: Éditions d'Art Albert Skira, 1960.

LASLETT, Peter, RUNCIMAN, W. G. and SKINNER, Quentin: *Philosophy, Politics and Society.* Oxford: Basil Blackwell, 1972.

LASSAIGNE, Jacques: *La Peinture espagnole, de Velásquez à Picasso.* Genève: Éditions d'Art Albert Skira, 1952.

MANDELBAUM, Maurice: *History, Man and Reason: a Study in Nineteenth-Century Thought.* Johns Hopkins University Press, 1971.

MARTIN, John Rupert: *Baroque.* Harmondsworth: Penguin Books, 1977.

MITTELSTRASS, Jürgen: 'Phaenomena bene fundata: from "saving the appearances" to the mechanization of the world-picture.' In R. R. Bolgar (ed.), *Classical Influences on Western Thought. AD 1650–1870*. Cambridge University Press, 1979.

PANOFSKY, Erwin: *Studies in Iconology*: Oxford University Press, 1939 (second edition 1962).

—: *Meaning in the Visual Arts*: Harmondsworth: Penguin Books, 1970 (first edition, London, 1955).

—: *Aufsätze zu Grundfragen der Kunstwissenschaft*. Berlin, 1964.

—: *La Prospettiva come 'forma simbolica' e altri scritti*. Milan: Feltrinelli, 1966; tr. by Enrico Filippini of the German original, Leipzig–Berlin, 1927.

PAPINEAU, David: *Theory and Meaning*. Oxford: Clarendon Press, 1979.

PODRO, Michael: *The Critical Historians of Art*. Yale Univetsity Press, 1982.

RITTERBUSH, Philip C.: *Overtures to Biology: the Speculations of the Eighteenth-century Naturalists*. New Haven: Yale University Press, 1964.

RUIZ-MIGUEL, Alfonso: *Filosofia y Derecho en Norberto Bobbio*. Madrid: Centro de Estudios Constitucionales, 1983.

SCHENK, Martin: *Uber den Umgang mit Geisteskranken: die Entwicklung der Psychiatrischen Therapie vom 'Moralischen Regime' in England und Frankreich zu den 'psychischen Curmethoden' in Deutschland*. Berlin: Springer, 1973.

SCHUMPETER, Joseph A.: *History of Economic Analysis*. Oxford University Press, 1954.

SCULL, Andrew T.: *Museums of Madness: the Social Organizations of Insanity in Nineteenth-century England*. PhD dissertation, Princeton University 1974.

SINGER, Charles: *A Short History of Scientific Ideas to 1900*. Oxford University Press, 1959. Paperback edition, 1962.

STANLEY, John (ed.): *From Georges Sorel: Essays in Socialism and Philosophy*. New York: Oxford University Press, 1976. Tr. by John and Charlotte Stanley.

STOVE, David: *Popper and After: Four Modern Irrationalists*. Oxford: Pergamon Press, 1982.

VENTURI, Franco: *Utopia and Reform in the Enlightenment.* Cambridge University Press, 1971.

WADE, Ira O.: *The Structure and Form of the French Enlightenment,* volume I: *Esprit Philosophique.* Princeton University Press, 1977.

WEIMANN, Robert: *Structure and Society in Literary History: Studies in the History and Theory of Historical Criticism.* London: Lawrence & Wishart, 1977.

WESTFALL, Richard: *Never at Rest. A Biography of Isaac Newton.* Cambridge University Press, 1980.

WILCOX, John T.: *Truth and Value in Nietzsche: a Study of his Metaethics and Epistemology.* University of Michigan Press, 1974.

YATES, Frances A.: *Giordano Bruno and the Hermetic Tradition.* London: Routledge and Kegan Paul, 1964.

Index of names

Fontana Modern Masters
Editor: Frank Kermode

Barthes
Second Edition

Jonathan Culler

Roland Barthes (1915–80) was an 'incomparable enlivener of the literary mind' whose lifelong fascination was with 'the way people make their world intelligible'. He has a multi-faceted claim to fame: to some he is the structuralist who outlined a 'science of literature', and the most prominent promoter of semiology; to others he stands not for science but for pleasure, espousing that literature which gives the reader a creative role. He championed the *Nouveau Roman* but his best known works deal with classic writers such as Racine and Balzac. He called for 'the death of the author', urging that we study not writers but texts; yet he himself published idiosyncratic books rightly celebrated as imaginative products of a personal vision.

Professor Culler elucidates the varied theoretical contributions of this 'public experimenter' and describes the many projects which Barthes explored and which helped change the way we think about a range of cultural phenomena, from literature, fashion, wrestling and advertising to notions of the self, of history and of nature.

In this new, updated version of his original study, Professor Culler has expanded the bibliography to include the latest works published by and about Roland Barthes, both in French and in English.

ISBN 0 00 686270 1

Fontana Press

Fontana Modern Masters
Series Editor: Frank Kermode

Lacan

Malcolm Bowie

In this Modern Master on Jacques Lacan (1901–81), Malcolm Bowie presents a clear, coherent introduction to the work of one of the most influential and forbidding thinkers of our century.

A practising psychoanalyst for almost fifty years, Lacan first achieved notoriety with his pioneering articles of the 1930s on Freud. After World War Two, he emerged as the most original and controversial figure in French psychoanalysis, and became a guiding light in the Parisian intellectual resurgence of the 1950s. Lacan initiated and subsequently steered the crusade to reinterpret Freud's work in the light of the new structuralist theories of linguistics. He evolved an elaborate, dense, systematic analysis of the relations between language and desire, focusing on the human subject as he or she is defined by linguistic and social pressures. His lectures and articles were collected and published as *Ecrits* in 1966, a text whose influence has been immense and persists to this day.

Lacan's thought was never stable: Malcolm Bowie traces the mutations in his critique of Freud, and explores the paradoxes and anomalies in his theories of sexuality. The volatility of his thinking comes under exacting scrutiny. For, in order to understand the work of many modern thinkers – literary theorists, linguists, psychoanalysts, anthropologists – knowledge of Lacan's revolutionary ideas, which underpin those of his successors across the disciplines, is indispensable. Malcolm Bowie's accessible critical introduction provides the perfect starting-point for any exploration of the work of this formidable thinker.

ISBN 0 00 686076 1

Fontana Press

Fontana Press

Fontana Press is a leading paperback publisher of non-fiction. Below are some recent titles.